White Hat Sales:
Building a White-Hot Business That Doesn't Burn You Out

by

Sandra E. LaFlamme

DORRANCE
PUBLISHING CO
EST. 1920
PITTSBURGH, PENNSYLVANIA 15238

Dorrance Publishing Co
585 Alpha Drive
Pittsburgh, PA 15238
Visit our website at *www.dorrancebookstore.com*

ISBN: 978-1-6366-1348-2
eISBN: 978-1-6366-1927-9

Contents

Introduction

The media says we are in trouble!

In fact you could say that the sorry truth about our culture is that our highly advanced technology system is generally used through the commercial and political agenda of mass media- to dumb down our culture. Unfortunately many of the sales practices and training not only dumb down sales people but encourage the dumbing down of consumers who do not always get a straight story when they want to buy a house or a car or some cosmetics. There is such a prevalent effort at manipulating people, despite their realization that they are being used, that many consumers have given up, and accept the half-truths, buy the good or service, and go home with a sense of defeat with sad eyes and sloping shoulders.

It's Time We Smarted Up!

White Hat Sales is all about waking up our culture to the value of integrity and truth in commercial interactions and to realize that if consumers, marketers, and salespersons would smart up, then our culture would be so much more perfected. And if the attitude of this level of integrity, coupled with self-knowledge but also about shrewdness about people and transactions, bled over into the American political landscape, why, we would soon be inching closer to fulfilling the goal of our Founding Fathers: liberty, integrity, and prosperity.

What does having a head injury and facing change have to do with the current state of affairs?

EVERYTHING!

Globally we have experienced the same events but all from a different perspective. When you experience a head injury, you don't know what you don't know.

With help a great community can facilitate a move. A move from knowing what you know to living what you know. A move from knowing what you don't know to knowing it and living it.

Doing this faster than you think you can by having strong examples. Pushing yourself from the inside out.

Since experiencing my head injury at ten, I have had years and years of migraines until the facial reconstruction with braces started in 2012. As of this writing in 2020, we are still making "adjustments." I am in the personal best shape of my life right now.

Thanks to scientific strategic changes in my physical, mental, and psychological well-being, I can demonstrate that my personality is not different, but my business and personal life have become radically more prosperous in 2020.

The head injury and the global change have something in common, I decided to succeed. I am writing to create community for those of us who decide to grow instead of complaining.

As antidote to this tragic distortion of American values, I have deliberately developed White Hat Sales with hope of creating a community in what you might call us the art-of selling niche. This is not merely to make a profit but also because I feel we need it.

Yes, our country! That we all feel, in our hearts, our country, the United States, should be a true beacon of light and liberty for all people, a paradigm that has grown and expanded in many ways since its origin, although often tainted by those who would put their predatory instincts above our people's natural passions for justice, equality, and liberty.

Right now we desperately need to return to that paradigm where we somehow left off and to restore the rightful place that free enterprise truly fits on the porch of liberty built so nobly by our Founding Fathers. After the early years of the Republic, smart and fervent American patriots, in efforts spread over several centuries, helped extend those critical economic and citizen rights to women, ethnic, and religious minorities.

But recently our citizens have been sold a bill of goods by politicians and special interest groups that degrade the rule of fair competition and true market value must occupy on that porch of personal liberty and commercial freedom. And unfortunately this "bill of goods" affects our trade policies, our defense postures, and gross domestic product as well as such small items, like unemployment, wages, healthcare, and citizen rights.

To restore that sense of balance, I believe we should use what remains unchallenged of our freedom of expression to explore various paradigm shifts, which have diminished our value for real freedom. Some clarity in doing this may be found in elements of human culture called mores and folkways as defined in modern sociology.

Mores distinguish the difference between right and wrong, while folkways draw a line between right and rude. Folkways are similar to what we generally speak of as "customs," the all-important norms for routine or casual interaction. This includes ideas about appropriate greetings and proper dress in different situations. Understanding these elements will enhance our ability to interact responsibly in other cultures, creating real communication and workable boundaries for commerce, civil liberties, military, and politics. To pursue our rights to commerce, we cannot overlook potential gaps in communication because of cultural misunderstandings.

Coping with the differences between our cultural conventions is a hallmark of the United States of America, and I believe we represent the finest leadership in the world for intercultural competence. The springboard here is to focus on these strengths and grow with the needs heard from consumers every day, the profile that comprises of every nationality from every continent. My approach to business has its origins in international real estate, and these concepts have been used effectively with every nationality from almost every continent.

In all of this, one paradigm that I am intimately involved with and that should not be neglected as a subset of an overall commercial enterprise paradigm is the significant and important activity of selling. "Selling," as generally thought of, involves the way we interact as companies and individuals with trading our goods and services mostly for currency. My current occupation as a realtor specializing in luxury homes is all about sales but in a highly innovative and effective way, a way that has produced a great deal of success.

As a strong and determined advocate of ethical and productive selling, I am writing this book because I want my readers to succeed in the way I have. As an active real estate sales practitioner, working every day in the field, as well as a successful blogger and journalist in this area, I am hoping through this book and related efforts in the La-Flamme Advanced Communication Training Community to pave the way for a major new paradigm of selling, useful for business owners, consumers, and professional sales people. I would like to see the concept and brand of *White Hat Sales and Marketing* discussed and debated in newspapers, schools, and in sales conferences. With this in mind, I offer it to you and to my country.

My own journey involved a discipline of self-mastery, a continual and ruthless examination of myself and an effort to transform myself into a person capable of conforming to a very high standard of personal conduct and a very successful performance in sales, which means maximizing profitability.

But let me be clear here.

Maximizing profitability through self-transformation does not mean learning to do whatever it takes to create profit for oneself or for one's company. Rather it means that having chosen a vocational path, in this case sales, I fully align myself with my chosen purpose in life in a way that allows me to function as a conscious person, motivated by essentially spiritual values in an often very, largely secular and economic world. This means that my ultimate goal is to serve not only my personal interests but my clients, the world around me, my clients, my country and, yes, in some way the entire planet. Human beings, by virtue of having been born in this world, have innately a lot of responsibility.

It has been my experience that perfecting my chosen occupation by aligning to purpose, defined in a spiritual and ethical sense, does not diminish profitability but maximizes sales performances and profit.

To this I have utilized certain concepts and techniques to change myself into a person fully aligned with purpose and to promote business and causes based on that transformation.

For this reason, and since the paradigm, I have formulated certainly trumps most conventional ideas about sales, I personally prefer as I have used previously, the label, "sales practitioner," over and above terms like sales person, salesman, or saleswoman.

If there is one thing I have done successfully, besides my (thank goodness!) rather robust customer service/sales record, it has been the wide-ranging success of my blogs, which have become traffic destinations for many new and established business people whose life and livelihood depends on sales. While this book certainly is influenced by my real estate experiences, all of that had foundations in the many sales activities I have engaged in the past. My past has been chockfull of all types of sales experience before and after I graduated from Iowa State University with a Bachelor of Science in Business in 1984.

When my parents converted their gas stations to convenience stores, I gained expertise in upselling at the cash register. This was a great skill to acquire, great for any high school student like myself who wanted advancement and opportunity.

When this happened, I already had a rather robust schedule of cleaning the barn before school, going to school, and afterschool cleaning countertops and driveways as a way to presenting a handsome image for our petroleum sales efforts.

Always keeping my goals in mind, including future clothes, band trips, and sports equipment, I readily enjoyed the employment of my time in a different direction with valuable new skills. My shift offered a chance to spread the word about timely opportunities on wiper fluid purchases during the rainy season as they were completing their gas and milk purchases. Because we were always in some sort of contest, I strove to learn upselling while adding cash rewards to my paycheck.

After graduation I began by working in management for Pittsburgh Paints on its implementation team for Utah, Idaho, Oregon, and Washington, handling retail and industrial sales from 1985 to 1986. My team sold to military, wholesale, and general contractors in the San Antonio areas. This began a long involvement in technical types of sales requiring a knowledge of various complex legal components and expected industry standards. In this case, I needed a knowledge of commercial and residential construction and was involved in obtaining governmental bids in public hearings, dealing with zoning committees and code enforcement. I think it provided me with a powerful introduction to complex corporate sales scenarios.

My next seven years were spent as a General Securities Representative for Transamerica. This again was a highly technical and legally sensitive form of sales but generally meant selling securities to individuals and was quite different than my work with Pittsburgh Paints. To really do this kind of a job, you needed an in-depth familiarity with domestic and international markets and the interrelationship between corporate entities and the various world of economies.

After a number of years, from 1993 to 2001, I was absorbed in technical software and computer training for Ohio Casualty, Atos Origin, and Gateway Computer, the only period of my career that sales was not an important, if not, the primary focus.

In 1999 I finally found a career path that fully satisfied my interest in an occupation that blended technical, legal, and interpersonal skills that was personally challenging, socially responsible, and potentially highly prosperous: finding people the right home. My enjoyment and success in my new career is probably indicated by participation in the All Star Rookie Team of Greater Cincinnati that very year. That level of success is also indicated when in 2016, I was able to found and become president of The National PTSD Service Association, an organization designed to provide highly trained service canines to Veterans and First Responders with PTSD.

In 1998 I took over a formidable task when I developed Manna Properties, supervising land development, including twenty-five residential property units, which I identified, refurbished, managed, and resold. This only happened because I had absorbed over my years in real estate an understanding of project flow in construction sufficiently to structure the job scope of sub-contractors, who I directed and coordinated during this process. I virtually shaped this project, so that sales would flow seamlessly. Prior to my formal beginning of this project, I had won the 2004 Commercial Preservation award from the City of Newport for my ability to conceptualize the best use of this property.

Now of course, my business as a global owner agent in real estate with eXpRealty is most satisfying and exciting. Given the challenging work of selling luxury homes, I wear my White Hat Sales Hat everyday, growing and prospering my clients, my team, and myself with care, honor, and integrity.

In this book, I'm determined to capture the seemingly enormous appeal my blog has had for so many. Its extraordinary response is probably a reflection of the deeper meaning I have brought to the ongoing Internet dialogue about real estate sales. Real, effective mentoring in any type of sales is of great value to serious business people all over the world.

But many times, unfortunately the actual reality of sales mentoring or coaching is often flawed. In this book, I want to provide a platform for that type of mentoring effort, as well as for directly influencing the methodology of sales carried out by the actual or prospective professional sales people in this audience.

Since White Hat Sales, as I describe it, involves what I call "transformation;" let me be clear that it embodies a personal development process that entails mindfulness, constructive reformation of your thought process, spontaneous empathetic analysis, and responsiveness to clients. It also involves the development of disciplined habits to parse and implement every component of the sales process, including price negotiations, development of contractual agreements, and other legally required documentation of a sale and many other elements that could be improved by association with a coaching or mentoring process, even through the written word.

The reality is that the insights in my blog and those developed in this book have substantially contributed to my success in my own sales and helped me achieve a particularly happy and satisfied real estate client base. This is further indicated by the many current and authentic testimonials in numerous valid, global Internet sites whose positive and nurturing comments have generated so many valuable leads.

In writing this book, I have tried to retain my natural style, similar to the successful way I have expressed myself in my various blogs and on Facebook. Still I am always looking to perfect the ease and clarity of my narratives, and no doubt you will assist in any further refinement which I accomplish. Your feedback is appreciated!

I hope to pay any feedback forward to you in some significant way, perhaps most importantly by communicating to you the essence of what I am saying in this book.

May your results be as big as mine for after first receiving some of the significant results I have recorded here, I had bigger sales in one month than all of the year past. Yes, that's what happened to me, just because I learned some of the secrets lying behind that simple two-letter word, N-O! I will explain the mystery of that word in the very next chapter and how understanding that mystery dovetails with everything I am trying to convey in this book.

But just to be sure, let us pause for just a moment to see if this book is something you can really use.

IS THIS BOOK FOR YOU?

- It would be, if you have clients, whatever profession you are in.
- If you have clients- yes, for sure.
- If you have an employer, he or she is going to experience big changes (even if he or she is not quite sure what they are).
- If you work/volunteer for a community organization, this book is for you.
- Getting started as a realtor? This book will jumpstart you in a big way.
- If you 're a burned-out realtor, this book may revive you.
- Out of work forever? Look for sudden positive changes in your job search.
- Off balance in work, this book can help get back on your tight rope.
- Want to move from management to sales? Start reading this book today!
- Do you want to have a global business as a real estate agent that comes with publicly traded stock?
  https://sandralaflamme.exprealty.careers/

Chapter 1

CLASSICAL FOUNDATIONS OF SALES SYSTEMS
and
The Need for a 21st Century Methodology

I am writing this book because I love sales.

Sales is an essential part of every culture, and believe me, I have been involved or witnessed that exciting activity in many places and in many cultures throughout the world. And in one sense, this book is a celebration of that process, which when directed properly, leads to great personal satisfaction in the world of both clients and sales practitioners. It is an honor to contribute to the literature of salesmanship, in what I hope is a sometimes novel but thoroughly useful way.

Commerce- A Basic Instinctual Drive for Reciprocal Sharing of Talent and Possessions

But before I go into the guts of the approach to professional sales developed in *White Hat Sales*, I would like to talk about the broader field that sales take place in: that of commerce.

Under the umbrella of commerce, I am including all those transactions where there is some kind of an exchange, some good or service for another good or service or various complex bundles of such goods and services, involving and including their surrogate cousin, sometimes called money or currency, as well as direct trade scenarios.

Commerce is a reciprocal urge to share talents and things. Charity is where you give freely without expecting a return. I submit that both of these are noble human instincts and their rightful deployment is regulated by divine law. That is to say, on the highest level, they are spiritual expressions of divine tendencies to prosper through sharing and to aid those in need to prosper by giving.

I firmly believe in both.

In my travels around the world, I believe I have confirmed to myself that human beings embody within themselves some essential instinctive sympathetic bond towards the possibilities of trade interactions, whether directly or through currency or direct barter, satisfying a very socializing need for people throughout the world. The giving and receiving of the products of labor seems to embody almost a universal understanding whatever form the transaction takes on.

During my 2000 mission trip to Kazakhstan, I witnessed that even the crippled street person, Igor, upon receiving the good news and manifestation of God's wholeness in his body, immediately sought wholeness in his finances. No one told him I was a business owner. He found me out of the sea of participants in my journey, and I communicated with him without ever speaking the same language. In this way, I was able to impart confidence to him that the very nature of our universe will draw him into a community of support and enterprise if he chooses. He wanted to be a business owner and understand some basics in sales. I believe I helped him and inspired him in his God-given wish.

Even the hotel, which I stayed, could assist me in transacting business twenty-four hours a day at their business center. I have found that I am always able to find a way to be connected, linked appropriately to the information I need, and be able to sell anywhere! And people are buying something somewhere all over the world.

But without this belief both in oneself, in the value of commerce and in the power of God, how would you know to <u>dig deeper</u> into how to assist a new but somewhat desperate person in your life? It took Igor just eight hours after I met him. In that short time, he was transformed from cripple, to healed man, to someone with a completely new view of the world looking to start his own business.

If, like Igor, you need help but don't know where to go to get it, whom do you ask but someone who's familiar with these important, wonderful processes? Right? It could be a friend, a motivational speaker, some kind of clergy, even an author.

The Critical Roles Sales
Plays in Commercial Activities

Sales are the side of commercial interactions that proposes some kind of an exchange.

And despite the bad light that is somewhat cast on the sales profession in the modern world, sales is an essential ingredient in our and other's culture and something that many, many people just love to do, and if they do, they would love to do it better. Sales can be a component in achieving the satisfaction of furthering wealth, security, enjoyment of life, and personal achievement, and of course, if done wrongly, the opposite of all those things. But in my book, *White Hat Sales*, I am on the happy side of sales, the good side.

· · · · ·

As a consumer, personally, how do you feel about the way sales are conducted in the United States? In comparison to other places in the world, where you may know about or have had some direct experience....?

· · · · ·

Integrity and Profitability-
To Some a Preposterous Idea

· · · · ·

I would love to have been a fly on the wall of your mind when each of my readers saw the title of my book, *White Hat Sales – Maximizing Profitability Through Self-Transformation.*

I am quite sure that there would be some prospective readers (hopefully just a few) that were repulsed by my "naïve" suggestion that sales should be totally honest and that the intention would always to put the client's interest before the sales practitioner, for whom this book is generally intended.

That prospective reader might also be incensed by our contention that LaFlamme Advanced Communication and the White Hat Sales System can maximize profitability with none of the toxic consequences for both client and sales practitioner possible with counterproductive Black Hat Sales scenarios that are illegal, immoral, or both.

The critics of our approach might say, "*Who are you kidding? White Hat Sales? Integrity? Empathy? Encouraging the client to look before he leaps? Not letting them make the wrong decision, even if it profits us? Anyone with this kind of attitude towards sales has signed a death warrant on their career.*" They also might add, "*In perusing some of your chapters, I have the impression you are trying to say there is a way to sell something without using real closing techniques. Why you should do that from the very beginning of the game! Are you crazy? Your clients will walk all over you. Actually probably just walk away.*"

Why would the skeptical prospective reader say this? Well, it's simple. That *annoyed title and book browser has the firm belief that the purpose of* sales is so you can take the money after confirming for sure that it is there and you have it- and run like hell. Life, these people would say, is brutal, and we need to get that money fast, no matter what.

They might also say, "*Don't you know that sales is a zero-sum game? * Win-win is a Pollyanna fantasy.*"

. . . . .

> **As a salesperson, have you ever violated your personal ethic in the way that you sell? Or if you belong to a slightly different school than the one you are checking out today, did you ever really have a sales ethic?**

. . . . .

---

*Definition of a Zero-Sum Game excerpt from Investopedia: "A situation in which one person's gain is equivalent to another's loss, so the net change in wealth or benefit is zero."

On the other hand, on the brighter side of the sales industry, a segment somewhat tinted with naiveté, there are other people who would say, "*I work in sales, and most of the people I know are honest. Why waste your time promoting honesty?*"

And for those astonished at my arrogant assertion about the prevalence of deception, I can only say, "Thank God for the little pockets of conscience and service-oriented people in this world," but that doesn't mean the rest of the world is like that. And further it doesn't mean that those really honest people know everything they need to know to maximize their profitability for themselves and others.

The reality is that this book, *White Hat Marketing*, is not just about honesty. It is about self-transformation, so that one can truly act with integrity; and integrity goes far beyond just telling the truth or being honest. As you will shortly see, if you keep turning pages, it is also about *making sure your client can hear you tell the truth*.

Reflexive vs Reflective Thinking- A Key to Our Sales Process

The White Hat Sales System is not just about making the tiny print clauses in a contract in giant fonts nor about shouting out the truth *but about making sure that the client's automatic, reflexive thinking does not impede him from hearing you and making the right decisions.* We don't want them to be guided by their largely reflexive impulses

Let me explain.

Reflexive thinking is fast thinking, as Nobel Prize Winner Daniel Kahneman points out in *Thinking, Fast and Slow*, his insightful book on the essential qualities of the human mind is fast, intuitive, and emotional and is the kind of thinking that often bypasses the valuable results of slower, reflective thinking, which is more deliberative and logical. There is value in both kind of thinking but bypassing reflective thinking can lead to some huge mistakes.

Do you get the difference between reflective and reflexive thinking; maybe because you're awed by its sharp, clean lines and nifty paint job or its ridiculously low price? It's somewhat like the difference between buying a used car without even looking under the hood and getting a great mechanic to check out all its systems first and then take you and it for a test drive. Do you try to buy reflectively, or do you always buy something, and twenty minutes later, regret it?

• • • • •

The White Hat Sales Program is about far more than just making the niceties of product disclosure. It is making sure that the client fully, consciously understands the benefits/pitfalls of what they are buying. This very hard because sometimes for often *the client is their own worst enemy.*

• • • • •

In your own sales practices, have you ever been consciously or philosophically concerned about what we have defined as reflexive thinking by yourself and your clients? Don't be concerned if you haven't? It doesn't come up in a lot sales systems.

• • • • •

That vulnerability, reflexive thinking (which is derived from the word, *reflex,* which implies an instinctive rather than a reflective response), is the core weakness that smart predatory sales agents act on. In fact predatory salespersons, in a live conversation, often will tell the truth, knowing that the client will miss their disclosure, sometimes because the catches on that their client may not be paying attention, but also because their conditioning and reflexive, unquestioned assumptions about some key issues are distracting them and driving them down the wrong path so powerfully that they are not responding rationally to what they actually hear.

• • • • •

> Have you ever steered a client away from a personally profitable sale because you felt it was not good for him? Did you feel elation, a sense of loss, or just a kind of satisfaction of making the right decision?

• • • • •

Black Hat vs White Hat Sales Methodologies

Black Hats can be very concentrated and very savvy, just as any hunters would be stalking their prey. Still although alert to their environment and the behavior of their target, they are asleep to their conscience and the common good. Perhaps even more sadly, they are indifferent to the real terms of their gift of life, which means cherishing the value and desires of other people outside of themselves.

White Hatters, who focus on the true reality of the upsides and downsides of their products, are certainly marching on the path to integrity, but there is more to our purpose in White Hat Sales than just integrity alone.

In White Hat Sales, although we want to truly help the client and that is paramount, White Hat Sales is not only about being honest but delivering a truly needed or desired product or service. In this sense, we are also strong advocates for what we have signed up for, our product or service, even if we have to stand up against what we believe is the reflexive resistance of our clients. It is not at all just about pleasing folks we are selling to. For this a sales practitioner needs to balance guts, determination, psychological strength and wisdom with the spiritual virtues of compassion, empathy, and a true desire to assist the client in fulfilling his or her actual goals.

Which bring us to why we developed White Hat Sales and the LaFlamme Community. We did this partially because we wanted to deploy some of these most recent discoveries of neuroscience in a positive way, as the kind of understanding derived from these discoveries can be useful to further clarity, equity, and mutual profitability in human interactions. But we also wanted to truly empower the sales practitioner.

A HUMANE PARADIGM FOR SALES NEEDS MORE THAN SCIENCE

The reality of science is that it is a tool that can be used to prepare a fallow field for bountiful resurrection to a powerful platform for organic crops in conjunction with the infusion of fresh compost, real plant nutrients, and fertile seeds from non-GMO plants. Tractors, seeders, threshers, and other equipment can be used to prepare the soil, plant, harvest, and process the plants, abundantly setting the stage for nurturing, healthful means. That same science that gives us modern vehicles and tools also gives us untested GMO seeds and plants, toxic pesticides, chemical fertilizers, and other elements that have jeopardized the purity of humanity's food pantry.

White Hat Sales looks at the productive uses of science in understanding the brain and human communication. To some extent, perhaps this will counteract the negative ways these neuroscience discoveries are being used in politics, in commerce, and in unlawful interrogation scenarios. Like everything else in this perplexing but fascinating world, potentially good science and technology can also be deployed selfishly and egotistically and in inarguably negative ways. A knowledge of cognitive mechanisms in the mind can be used to take advantage of certain weaknesses found to exist in human neurophysiology, weaknesses that were built into our nature no doubt to protect us from quick and dangerous adversaries, which, in fact they sometimes still do. But we don't have to be victims of these protective mechanisms. Understanding their role in our psyches is critical to gaining control over our own reflective powers, but also we can productively use our genuinely intuitive powers and recognizing the times when "fast thinking" can save our life and fortune.

· · · · ·

Have you ever practiced Black Hat Marketing consciously or inadvertently? What have you practiced that you think might have been Black Hat, and how did you relate to those practices retrospectively? Was there ever a point where you doubted the efficacy or morality of one or more sales training systems?

· · · · ·

Does Cognitive Persuasion and Trance Induction Have a Place in Salesmanship?

There have been two main sides to sales training in the twentieth century. One has been more or less White Hat, stressing techniques of sales based on a shrewd assessment of people's characters and proclivities. The interactions would generally present a strong case for all the benefits offered by the product or service followed by attempting to lead the client to the value of an immediate purchase by persistent questioning, all the while looking for an opening to close the sale before the sales practitioner's presentation was technically over. This was White Hat tending towards gray perhaps because the product was presented honestly with good intentions by the sales practitioner but still involving an edge of manipulation based on a kind of subtle adversarial posture by the sales practitioner towards the client.

The Black Hat side of marketing was based on partial, total, and sometimes toxic deceptions about product, price, and utility relying on cognitive persuasion, a form of story telling developed by shrewd sales operators before its neurological basis had been discovered. The techniques, which I am calling cognitive persuasion, are in fact a methodology as old as the hills. Then there was also trance induction, a subtle form of hypnosis developed by Milton Erickson, and modified, accelerated, and implemented in sales training through neurolinguistic programming techniques, commonly known as NLP. More about that later.

Rackham's Breakthroughs in Sales Paradigms

When we look at the development of technology, particularly recently with the rise of social media and mobile technology, we see how quickly paradigms can shift abruptly.

The history of mankind has seen massive paradigm shifts in technology, political systems, cultural interfacing, and the way commerce works. One of those shifts, surprisingly new, is the systematic development of sales skills. Here is one short historical sketch by a professor who is an innovator and author himself in the development of sales systems.

In an interesting introduction to the book, *The Challenger Sale: Taking Control of the Customer Conversation* by Mathew Dixon and Brent Adamason, Professor Neil Rackham, himself the author of *SPIN Selling*, another best-selling book on sales, enumerates four major historical breakthroughs in sales paradigms:

1. When insurance companies gave up compelling their sales people to split their focus on collections, which eventually compromised their time to sell and split collections and sales into different functions, with entirely different groups of employees take charge of their specialty. The manifestation of this was the hunter/farmer

strategy with the sales practitioners being the hunters and the collectors the farmers, mainly harvesting the cash and providing some maintenance contact. This took place in the very early twentieth century.

2. The second breakthrough was E. K. Strong's book, *The Psychology of Selling*, which for the first time identified and explained basic skills in sales, involving techniques like closing, handling objections, explaining features and benefits, etc. It basically jumpstarted the sales training process.

3. The third breakthrough he credits is his own, called SPIN Selling, the name of his own book, written in 1988. It focused on the way to sell complex products, introducing new, sophisticated models capable of handling these more daunting challenges for making sales.

4. Rackham claims the fourth breakthrough is the Challenger Sales concept, which he is introducing in the beginning of *The Challenger Sale* book. This focuses on five categories of sales people, which Rackham believes has been extracted with great care by the researchers who formulated the basis of Dixon and Adamson's book. They are the hard worker, the challenger, the relationship builder, the lone wolf, the reactive problem solver.

The Challenger Sale, first published in 2011, based on extensive research, presents a new and exciting 21st century paradigm for sales. The challenger concept is empirical, based on an understanding that requires empathy, very advanced understanding of a client's own product or service, and an intuitive ability to see the client's true needs before the client sees them, coupled with a desire to serve. This is neither a docile nor an essentially psychologically manipulative role and is seemingly a productive contribution to 21st century White Hat marketing.

Perhaps the big surprise Rackham presents is the declining of the idea of relationship sales as being in the forefront of sales methodologies. According to the challenger sale, "liking" the sales rep comes more or less after liking what he does in providing the kind of answers to specific problems or opportunities that the client might have.

The Challenger Paradigm-
A Winning Prototype for Complex Sales Packages

Often contemporary sales require customized solutions and therefore entails "solutions sales" as opposed to "product sales." The tools I have within the very framework of ExpRealty give me the ability for my clients to be introduced to me, to connect with me, and to like me and to trust me. Technology exists to propel the human product, so if you are good, you must use the "NOW" technology. I don't use the rotary dial phone to make calls. I use the latest product on an excellent network. Product knowledge is not enough. In every industry, there exists a disrupter because they are meeting a human need with tools that are more fulfilling for recipients and the delivery person. In my case, I am a business owner and a delivery person. To some I am just a rep, until I help them become part of my community.

Firstly the rep has to be smart enough to be able to formulate very specific solutions for the client. But to really succeed in these efforts, his or her profile must conform to the characteristics of the challenger category of sales rep. Here are some of the qualities needed according to Dixon and Adamson's book:

#1 You must have deep insight into the customer's business, perhaps even what they understand at the moment.

This needs to be sufficient that you can point out solutions that often they never thought of, including using those solutions to indicate a winning strategy using the very products or services you are selling. The authors call this a "boardroom-level of engagement with customer." To do this, they must "teach, tailor, and take control."

#2 You must be aggressive enough to take a stand on initiatives you believe are in your client's interest, even if you have to stand-alone.

Unlike relationship sales, which fosters a buddy-buddy type of relationship, making the customer happy to interact with the rep, this kind of challenger sale interaction is disruptive and may require a powerful sense of tact, diplomacy, and outright aggressive forwardness to push a mass of stakeholders into a new framework of thought about the company's direction and strategy. To this end, they must build a consensus, a network of advocates from a variety of significant stakeholders, to make this work. They must let their own borders, based on product knowledge, often extend beyond their customers.

#3 You need to teach and therefore lead, foregoing previously expected roles as an account executive from a vendor organization.

The role is more like a master teacher than a researcher, the kind of teacher that rivets your attention and floods your mind with new idea rather than the one that compels you to aimlessly doodle while his voice morphs into a slow, background hum. Advice built out of phrases like "cutting cost, increasing revenue, opening into new markets, mitigating risks" in unexpected and exciting ways will magnetize their attention and create supplier/sales rep retention.

Certainly not all sales require this level of skill, technical knowledge, and leadership, but the essence of forward-looking, knowledgeable, and empathic sales is certainly compatible with our own paradigm. But the clients that face challenger salespeople are probably a bit more sophisticated than clients in other types of sales, but they appear to be generally moving in the White Hat area: to serve, not to manipulate for the sake of self-interest.

But sometimes service requires *chutzpa* and stepping out to take leadership. And in White Hat Sales, this kind of *chutzpa* is necessary when you take on the irrational narratives of a client's deeply hidden and often unconscious assumptions about a transaction.

· · · · ·

> By virtue of your expertise in your product, do you ever open new vistas for your clients? Do you try to think proactively and innovatively about what you are selling? Do you have enough knowledge of your own product or service to be able to think in this way? Do you think this type of effort is worthwhile, and if you had that type of knowledge, would you be willing to communicate it, even if you thought initially that there might be substantial resistance from the Stakeholders.

· · · · ·

Salespeople as Well as Consumers
Need to Be Rescued from the Dark Side of Sales

Yes, there were many great sales training and sales techniques that evolved towards the creation of organized and fairly ethical sales activities. There is a legacy of positive moments and ideas in the history of sales.

But that is not the case for many sales practices, which are firmly grounded in the dark sides of sales, some of which whose origins are clearly in the twentieth century or before. And many of these are truly alive and well today. I believe many of these salespeople, trained initially by the perpetuators of these practices, often feel trapped in a fog of conscience vs unfairly achieved profit, clarity vs being a willful creator of a minefield of illusions.

For these basically well-intentioned but poorly trained salespeople whose work is in modalities where deception runs rampant, White Hats Sales will bring a refreshing difference into their lives and careers. For them our approach, which promises profitability with integrity, will be a path of true liberation.

A New, Blessed Sales Paradigm for the Consumer

But now imagine how a typical American consumer, now suspicious and battle-hardened, will react to a sales practitioner when that consumer knows the sales practitioner is familiar with and committed to White Hat Sales techniques, possibly even certified by one of our future programs? How will that disenfranchised client react to a program that puts the client first in front of the sales practitioner or his or her agent?

Through our books and workshops, we are developing a sales training and mentoring program as a brand trumpeting an approach to selling and marketing that coheres with true respect for the consumer. Our techniques, philosophy, and their implementation will emphasize integrity and empathy in selling. For the American consumer, it will certainly serve as an antidote to the shady way so many goods and services are marketed and sold in this country. It will also overshadow the more mellow, somewhat ethically ambiguous techniques of Gray Hat Sales, sales that may strongly emphasize the power of the sales practitioner over the client but are not drenched in outright deception or even, as we will discuss, Black Hat covert trance induction.

I guess you can say that with *White Hat Sales*, a book and platform which conforms to the standards of my larger system under development, the LaFlamme Advanced Communication Training, I am creating an iconic type of sales approach for the 21st century. Perhaps in that way the American people can understand better what a reliable approach to sales is and prevent their further victimization, reaching now into every level of commerce but also into the core of their political life and even social life.

Politicians are often selling a bill of goods to their constituents at strategic political moments, which they doubtless do not intend to keep, dragging us into dubious domestic and international policies by deception and outright untruths. But although we cannot go into this issue here, we can only say that sales techniques are not confined to commerce and have significantly affected the morale and destiny of this nation.

Chapter 2

WHITE HAT SALES
The Next Dimension in Client-Sales Practitioner Interactivity

The current reality of sales is that, generally speaking, sales practitioners are usually trying to convince clients to buy from them. Clients are not generally begging sales practitioners to sell to them, although frankly it happens every day under certain circumstances (<u>antiques and collectibles, real estate, business broker transactions, etc</u>).

But since we are looking at things from the sales practitioner's perspective, we must ask, what does it take to be qualified for the enviable position of helping a consumer decide between their hard-earned money and your commodity?

The meaning and emotional sense of buying changes from time to time. In our era, considering our worldwide financial banking crisis (except for Canada and Australia, who actually enforce their banking laws), America no longer has as many consumers robbing Peter to pay Paul with bank funds. Buying things is more generally through our citizens' own hard-earned money, involving long hours at work, sometimes two or three jobs. Double duty.

Trust — The Vital Foundation
Of Client Relationships

What qualifications and accreditations do you need to have? Why should they trust you?

If you are interested in navigating in these rough waters of selling, get used to asking this question of yourself every time you have an exchange. What are the tools that will help someone to believe you and, more importantly, believe *in* you?

Sales, bottom line, is a form of negotiation, and negotiations can be conducted with a wide variety of demeanors on both sides, suspicion, trust, anger, affection, cruelty, kindness, the list of possibilities is endless. But when you talk about a sales approach that engenders trust, that narrows down the field of possibilities. Certain behavior does not lead to that kind of happy bonding with a client.

For that reason, in White Hat Sales, trust is the key factor we wish to engender in our clients. But we are not going to just project trust; we are going to actually be trustworthy. And beyond that, in our interactions with people, we will be who we are actually are, our personae somewhat logically customized to the person and circumstances we are dealing with as anyone would, given the wide range of human personalities and situation, but essentially and authentically always being ourselves.

As Polonius says to his son Laertes in Shakespeare's *Hamlet*, "This above all: to thine own self be true and it must follow, as the night the day, Thou canst not then be false to any man."

And beyond simply heeding that sage advice, we are going to equip ourselves with the tools that will enable our clients to make good decisions based on an enlightened, rational view of the product or service they are buying. When we close the sale, it is going to be win-win on both sides but not just for thirty days. Indeed for the expected or guaranteed life of the product or service, it will be what the client thought it was during the sales process. No tricks to haunt the sales practitioner's reputation at a later date.

• • • • •

> What kind of efforts have you made to establish trust between yourself and your clients? Does a unique situation have to come up to engender that trust, or can your trustworthiness be somehow demonstrated in the course of ordinary negotiations? Are you willing to lose the account altogether if you tell the client some of your true concerns? In what sense does this kind of effort require investing some kind of trust in source and the way the universe actually works?

• • • • •

Trust but Gumption

But just because we are White Hat, and want to project trust based on authenticity, does not mean we do not want the sale. Our job is to get the sale, if it is appropriate, and in entirely the right way.

To do that, we are willing to penetrate the veil of deception that often pervades the experience of negotiations where fear, greed, and illusion sometimes dominate. To that end, we are willing to challenge the client's assumptions and way of thinking if we need to. To that end, we are willing to do the kind of things that lead to a decision, including sometimes piercing the obstacles thrown up that are based on unrealistic, unfair, or self-destructive assumptions, habits, or beliefs of the client. This is somewhat like the challenger sales protocol. We want to have our practitioners show positive, demonstrative action based on truth and reality, to benefit the client, even if at first, or even later, it feels alienating.

If the car runs a lot better than it might in twenty minutes, if the desk looks shiny and new but the laminated top is made out of inferior material, if the stock looks golden to a bunch of well-respected financial analysts, but you have done your homework and you demur, this is the White Hat signal to put the truth before the sale.

White Hat Sales is a combination of very tough and very gentle thinking. It is contextual sales that sometimes requires extreme firmness or extreme kindness. And although we believe in tact, honesty, and patience does not mean we have to be wimps.

You need gumption. Yes, you do.

Although this book is about selling as a sales professional, negotiating to get something in exchange for some thing else, the art-of-the-sale is embedded in our lives in many different ways. Even in our jobs, there are aspects of in-house selling and negotiating that will affect our promotions, our raises, and our overall satisfaction.

For some a careful consideration of selling yourself to a prospective employer or what you want from your employer or colleagues at work may give some interesting clues as to what is involved in professional selling.

If you want an office with a window, you may have to sell your boss on it. If you want to extend the deadline for that special report, you better be prepared to chat up the reasons. If you want a bigger Christmas bonus, be prepared to do a lot of selling, assuming you dare to bring it up at all.

Ignorance, weakness, and downright stupidity often clouds negotiations.

The fact is you can be a professional athlete and not know how to negotiate your salary. Leaving the salary negotiation up to your manager may be renouncing to exercise a rather elementary but critical skill personal set that takes some fewer years to understand than it does to learn how to shoot a free throw. I think I learned both at about the same time. Asking for money to mow lawns and playing back yard hoops with my brother.

· · · · ·

> In what sense is being aggressive about the value of your product appropriate? Is it ever appropriate? If so how would you describe that kind of aggressive behavior if you yourself were deploying it in a presentation or negotiations with a client?

· · · · ·

Key Moments and Hard Questions

Some salespeople are good at calculated care. They go step-by-step in life, nurturing plants, pets, and people, even their clients, even when embarked on a sales career. Very good at displaying caring. But not so good perhaps when calculating a good time to ask hard questions, questions needed at key moments if you are going to be an effective sales practitioner. Questions THAT SHOULD BE ASKED!

First to ourselves. People who are otherwise meticulous, framing out discussions and minor considerations with skill and accuracy but then stumble at important points. Perhaps like a super achieving, consistently meticulous, and inventive NASA engineer who flounders dangerously and then retreats when faced with the opportunity to ask for the job opportunity they really want.

Sometimes the most important questions to ask are the ones that help you the most:

- Ring up the purchase.
- Close the deal.
- Ask to be hired.
- Ask for the job.

- Request profit-sharing with bonus for exceptional sales.
- Ask for a referral.
- Ask for the name and number of the keen friends of clients.

Why might a person falter at this moment? There are a variety of interesting reasons. The main one is fear, and fear has many faces.

The fact is when you ask for the sale, or the job, you are reaching for a decisive moment. And what if the client or the boss says no? That's it. It's all over with.

As we shall explore here later, actually a first, second, or third no, if actually challenged, can be the beginning of a negotiation and not the end.

But if you don't realize that, then you might be afraid of hearing the first one.

But as I said, fear has many faces.

And perhaps the worst one is receiving an actual final no that will alter the desired picture of your future, in a big or little way.

Facing that possibility could in fact keep you from pitching your need for the moment or for a long time to come, if ever.

As we shall discuss, that type of procrastination is based on scripts or narratives in your mind, including one that overwhelmingly is afraid of losing an opportunity because of someone else's decision. The ironic thing about your own inner scripts is that they are preventing you from quickly assessing your client's potential scripts and judging whether his no is spontaneous and reflexive or if it is truly reflective, correct, and in fact, meritorious.

When you hear a no, it is time to act, even if the initial action is only one of heightened awareness and analysis. And with a no, there needs to be a dual target: the client and yourself!

• • • • •

> Why is handling no so important in the sales profession? In the past, when you have received a no, how have you handled it? Did you, over a period of time, evolve to a different perspective on no before reading this book, or has it generally been the same since you started selling. Before you continue to read further, what is your inner reaction to no, and how do you interact with your client when you hear it?

. . . . .

HANDLING THE NO IN SALES
~ A SOMEWHAT OBLIQUE EXAMPLE ~

I like to look at job hunting and job positioning as examples of sales. Some would say this is a somewhat oblique example, but it really isn't. Job hunting and positioning are very good examples of sales because:

1) Because they are.
2) Because everyone has experienced this type of interaction.
3) Because almost everyone has had disappointments and challenges in this area making the actions involved easier to look at from a psychological sales standpoint.

Let us take an example that hypothetically might be involved with you and your job (even if it is quite different than the job you really have):

Just for fun, let's pretend you are someone who decides to ask for a different position in his or her company, perhaps a promotion. You saw the position listed on the company's bulletin board and you know you can ace the job.

You make an appointment at the department manager's office. You make sure to arrive on time and have a speech prepared, but when it comes to ask for the position you came for, you falter.

Do you falter because they may say no?

Many times it may be. But it can also be the opposite. Maybe they will say yes.

This is where a lightening self-examination may be necessary.

One reason your needed question can be difficult to ask is that you lack confidence to ask it. That may be because although you want something specific new, you really have not unraveled the long-term outcomes are looking to achieve.

Somewhere underneath the part of you that is about to ask, there may be a narrative like this:

> *You know, if I ask for the job, I may actually get it. And looking at Larry Hayworth, who just quit, it may be because although the pay is great, but the hours are horrendous.*

> *Or*

> *What am I doing here? I love my job, and although the pay is great and the title is superior to mine, this job is just a job in complex record-keeping with a tiny bit of legal knowledge thrown in to help with the analysis of certain targeted situations. I have always loved marketing, but this is like mentally digging ditches with a GPS unit to help me locate where I should dig. Boring!*

Of course there could be many more examples. Perhaps as many as grains of sand on the beach or as many people on this over-populated planet. Well, getting back to you, the hypothetical applicant, although some narratives may take quite a lot of digging to turn up, there also ones that you really know about, but for one reason or another, you have ignored. These are narratives that are compelling you not to say anything

Why are you there then? It is because you have been guided by other narratives that have come to the forefront of you mind, starting when you were standing at that bulletin board and are now still dominating, pushing you into that office, demanding you get another job. For instance maybe when you looked at the bulletin board, you said to yourself:

> *This dream job of mine is great. I have so many friends in the marketing department and each assignment is challenging. Just look at how many awards I amassed in two years. I am a super star but unfortunately a poor one. I still am all right, but my credit cards are screaming out to me to buy a few more groceries, to get that dishwasher I still can't afford. Still I know I will hate this stupid job if I happen to get it.*

> *Or*

> *I love my job, but I know my new boss hates me. She is envious of my work and goes out of her way to try and find anything outside of my work to lecture me about: five minutes late for work, leaving out a small part of my latest report, even daring to tell me not to talk too much to my partner in my little cubbyhole. I don't want to make a formal complaint. Maybe it would be best to go to the compliance department where the work is boring, but I know all the employees there, and they will definitely mind their own business.*

So just at the moment you are applying, you are feeling the weight of narratives that were just barely registering in your conscious mind when you were staring at the bulletin board.

And since one of these narratives is now asserting itself, while you are standing there in the office about to make a pitch, you now have a feeling that the request is premature. You do not feel confident about your footing.

In an actual business sale, it could be that you had developed a negotiation and endgame that maybe you weren't sure of. Maybe there were factors about the value of the antique or the workability of the used dishwasher you were selling that you were not sure of. Maybe your conscience was bothering you.

But being ambivalent about a new job or new position is not unusual. What is odd is how little people realize how much they are divided within about this kind of situation and thousands of others. It just isn't all that easy being a human being.

And we sales practitioners are human beings, aren't we?

A New Enlightenment

According to George Lakoff, a specialist in cognitive linguistics, a science which encompasses matching specific uses of language with the activity in the brain, you cannot make a strictly logical decision without bringing your emotions into play. In fact he speaks of a New Enlightenment, "a deep rationality that can take account of, a mind that is largely unconscious, embodied, emotional, empathic, metaphorical, and only partly universal."[1]

Taking it deeper to the nature of my writing, you are choosing the thoughts that nurture your emotions. Your free will is guiding you. If you disagree that you have free will, the mere fact that you debate this is evidence of your free will and will probably bring a laugh or a slam of the book down. Emotional, aren't we?

Getting back to you as the applicant standing in your boss's office, the consequences of you asking for a job just because it is available and you can do it, or because you have pre-planned a monetary offer for a sale could be momentous and possibly very unpleasant. Depends on the job or what you are selling.

Looking for a new job or new position in your company might require some deep reflexive thinking after a bit of real fact finding. Sometimes you may be tempted to wander outside or below your real skill set. There is a risk involved in that. Also, just making a decision about a price doesn't necessarily mean it should be coming off the top of your head. It needs to be researched and reflected on, depending of course on what you are selling.

The reality is that many organizations have processes and procedures written down to tasks achieved every fifteen minutes. Employees in these places usually are holding their first job. The documentation folks who write these management manuals have vast experience in product and employee wage profitability. When these protocols for implementation fail, the business fails, and there are no longer any jobs.

When you are afraid to ask for the type of job that suits your skill set, you are exposing yourself to the minimum level of security, even a place without security altogether. Completely placing your future ability to contribute your gifts and talents in the hands of someone who only knows you by your employee I.D. can be very scary. And often when this opportunity presents itself, you have no more room to negotiate than a smoke break.

Each level that you take to learn the process and procedures of the organization or industry where you work or where you may work, you are creating an opportunity to sell yourself. So one reason you may be faltering in a proposing a change in your job is that you haven't fully assessed where that job will take you. Further you may not know where it will take your employer. Will you fail him because you don't really like it because it contradicts certain career directions you have fantasized about because you may not like the working conditions around him, which you currently know nothing about?

When you make a decision, if you feel uncertain, examine the narratives that may lie behind it.

This is also true when you are selling a commodity or service. You really should be assured that what you are selling has a value that you are behind. You should also be relatively sure of your price.

Reflecting brings calmness and rewards.

· · · · ·

Why is applying for a job a good paradigm for understanding how you should sell products or services to clients? List some of the sales skills involved when you seek employment or have an interview? Compose a successful narrative about yourself and your qualifications for a job of your dreams.

· · · · ·

If you are selling multi-level products as I have done, an error involving accidentally misrepresenting a few hundred-dollar sales or realizing that they are overpriced in the marketplace, considering what they really are, will not hurt you. But if you are in my business, selling a million-dollar home, the financial and personal consequences of making any kind of a mistake can be significant.

If you are facilitating a merger for a large amount of money or selling your company, it is not just your finances at stake but also your future value of your current investment, financial freedom, integrity, business sense, and overall reputation.

EXCUSES BEGONE!

One truly fascinating book is Wayne Dyer's *Excuses BeGone!*[2] This book provides a methodology for self-transformation based on "right thinking," which includes the belief that habits that are excused by so-called genetic obstacles, a poor sense of self-esteem, professed failures in the past, the feeling that lack of money is an unconquerable barrier to achieving one's goals are the kind of poppycock you need to give up.

Sales practitioners have a lot of excuses for failure, but some of the worst is that they leave out necessary steps in introducing themselves to prospective clients.

> **If your goal is to operate on a professional level-**
>
> 1. **You must be able to briefly explain your benefit.**
>
> 2. **To pay attention to the head, eye, and body movement of your counterpart**
>
> 3. **To have a calm reserved understanding within yourself knowing the process and procedures which will work for your client.**

Exhibiting avariciousness or impatience in your presentation and failing to ask questions to get a sense of your client will also limit your success and lower the average sale price of the product or service you find yourself transacting.

I can assure you the bar is very high for someone who wants to be White Hat in their approach to sales. I am sure Wayne Dyer would agree with the thought that one of the most important things is to bring awareness or mindfulness into one's sales activities.

A novice in sales may be well-intentioned, but without practice and commitment, good intentions are never enough.

Even in a good-hearted attempt to encourage the client to be reflective, there is the problem that the sales practitioner, no matter how well meant their intention, may miss valuable clues and needs of the potential clients, simply because the sales practitioner, him or herself, is not sufficiently knowledgeable about self.

Sales practitioners miss the signals in others because they miss signals in themselves, signals indicating that they may be pre-judging the clients, emotionally over-valuing the price of the product because of a desire for the sale, refusing to acknowledge that some element of the transaction is a problem because it will require some time-consuming research.

One of the main problems for White Hat sales practitioners could be a lack of attention to critical elements in our process. For instance being neglectful of making a sufficient conscious attempt to empathize with the client, a quality which, when activated, can produce understanding and sympathy of the client's point of view, help foster the use of language or jargon that resonates well with the client, help provide a clear understanding of the client's cultural habits, specifically in relationship to negotiations, as well as giving you a better understanding of his or her emotional relationship to finances.

To accomplish better and more productive results with clients, this book presents an introduction to various practical self-transformation protocols and methodologies, which will allow the sales practitioner to transform his interactions with the client by transforming himself.

END NOTES

1. George Lakoff, *The Political Mind*, (Viking, New York, 2008) 14

2. Wayne Dyer, *Excuses Begone!* (Carlsbad, CA: Hay House, 2009)

Chapter 3

THE COGNITIVE FOUNDATIONS OF SALES NARRATIVES
PUTTING THE 'KNOW' IN 'NO'

I remember waking up underwater, feeling no pain, and thinking, "Mom will kill me if I die this way."

The rest is blurred, except for a significant flash forward as I recall having an ice pack on the back of my head while profusely apologizing to Mom for hurting myself. Everything else about the rest of that trip only draws a blank.

No Diving

That was the largest phrase on a relatively short list of the pool rules that could be read, printed on a sign, from twenty yards away. But the big scar on the back of my head has produced is a demonstrated ability active to this day – to *not* read "NO" in the wrong way. I should have taken that NO seriously, or I wouldn't have experimented with a back flip that made me wind up with a busted head.

As I learned back then, it was not appropriate to *hear* or *read* "NO" in the same gentle manner my mom meant during that beautiful Colorado vacation day way back when I was ten years old. "No!" she proclaimed. I would not be permanently injured or even die because of my inappropriate acrobatics on the board. "No!" I would not spoil the rest of their vacation. "No!" I would never, never do that again and give my family so much grief.

That's the last time I did that maneuver without more caution.

A busted sales deal is what motivates caution now. For years, whenever that happens, I always ask myself, what factors busted up my sale? What caused my client to say NO...? Was it something inappropriate I said? Was it my approach to the sale? Was it that I pushed too hard or that I hardly pushed at all?

I take NOs seriously now!

When this situation pops up with a client, all I can think about until I find the answer is how could I have busted up that NO?

. . . . .

> For a moment, go back into your own childhood. What lessons did you know about listening carefully to no in the real world. Did the universe, as in my case, send you a good strong lesson, and if so, how did this affect your future behavior? Why do we emphasize no so much? Why is handling no so important in the sales profession?

. . . . .

This book is all about the answers I have found after making mistake after mistake. With those answers, my sales have accelerated, and as I have mentioned, the happiness factor of my clients have dramatically increased.

The Hidden Narratives Behind No!

<u>Part of our inner work to develop our sales expertise</u> is to find the hidden narratives or meaning behind the no.

This is not a simple, automatic process. Yes, we know the brain does react to narratives, which are "mental" stories that follow a logical process. And we know that some narratives instinctively have more weight than others, a factor that can interfere with careful, reflective thinking.

Does every no or lightning quick response represent a definitively structured narrative in the brain? Yes! If you hear no as an opportunity and it makes you feel engaged, challenged, and happy, or it makes you feel rejected, a failure, and victimized, both emotions are housed in your brain structure and circuitry. Making good choices and helping others make good choices are housed in your amygdala and hippocampus.

The amygdala and hippocampus part of your brain and their connected circuits do this for you. Passion and perceptual emotions are dealt with by the amygdala. Memory and motivation are dealt with by your hippocampus. Even though you can't always control your circumstances, you can make fundamental choices that will help you control your reaction to your circumstances and keep toxic input out of your brain.

We need to be pro-active and identify that big bad NO before it busts up our sales. But to do that, we need to know all about that word, NO, its multiple uses, its good and bad contexts (like what my mother said when I hurt myself in the pool), when the sales practitioner should use the word and when the sales practitioner should almost pretend they are deaf when they hear it (and keep moving along the track even though the dreaded NO word was uttered).

We need to bust up the big bad NO, but we also need to embrace and understand some of its nicer and even very sympathetic cousins.

• • • • •

> Why do you suppose our brains seems to hide certain narratives that so strongly influence our behavior? If they are so hidden, how do you suppose they can be found? Do you think you can learn to substitute a nurturing narrative for a negative, destructive one?

• • • • •

Yes, there are different varieties of no you need to understand if you are in sales. You want to bust those big bad nos but you need to embrace a lot of those little ones. And some of those nos will need to be said to customers from time to time.

> In your sales efforts, what was the worst big bad no you have ever experienced? Do you think, in retrospect, you could have pro-actively prevented it? How did you handle it back then? How would you handle it now? What do you think you would need to know to handle it more effectively in the future?

Every matter-of-fact statement, every "truism," is not always applicable. There is a context to everything. We need to know what actions and states of mind can disassemble a great sale and make it fall apart. In this way, we can create a higher probability of success.

• • • • •

> **In the course of a sales presentation, how do you handle a no when it could lead to a final rejection of the sale? How do you handle a big bad final no emotionally? How do you want the client to think you are reacting? What about your current thoughts and behavior would you like to change?**

· · · · ·

We need to keep in mind that this is a rapidly changing world, and since both technology, communication, and motivation factors are also constantly changing, we need to face that reality when we do our business with clients who express their needs and motivations differently than they did even a few years ago. Based on the tremendous improvement in my business, I believe the following fundamental insights can help anyone.

One thing we must not ignore is the way people interact with each other and the way they transact business. Almost all of us realize that life has changed somewhat since social networking, and mobile phones demand more and more of our time and have altered the kinds of relationships we have, but have we really examined the impact of these changes and integrated it into our decision-making?

In my child-like way, I ignored what the swimming pool rules said and didn't give a microsecond to the consequences of not obeying them, particularly that one about diving. Let's not ignore all the wisdom about the real world that surrounds us, available to use if we are willing to look. And as for social media and mobile phone communications, that's just the visible part. We need to be aware of all the stuff we can't see, technological changes or not.

That is what the LaFlamme Advanced Communication Training is all about, the invisible component communication in a world in which the residents have 95% of their emotions and thought practices acting automatically on their behalf, where it takes an extra effort to resist easy inclinations and snap decisions. This is the reality that neuroscience has presented to us, a world where the light of reason shines through layers and layers of gray and black narrative filtering.

MARKETING TO THE SICK AND INFIRM

What do I mean by this?

We have been looking at inner narratives, many being extremely fast, perhaps a legacy of more prehistoric times when our actions were considerably more dependent on the instinct to survive. In epochs of time before the written word, before math and science, before a sophisticated political life, we needed our instincts to survive. Better eat than be eaten.

Some inner narratives are cautionary. They tell us to hold the fort and therefore that might be a good thing. They may be reflexive in a sense, but they are giving us room to reflect. Other narratives are instinctive reactions to things that sound good but are not based on analysis and reflection, so they could lead us to good things but also to things that only appear to be good but then could be very bad.

The challenge of marketers who only care about their product and not their consumer base (except for their pockets) is to find a way to overcome negative narratives by triggering positive ones.

Take a look at pharmaceutical ads. Where they warm you up by telling you about some wondrous solution to your diabetic blood sugar problem and they show an attractive young lady on a swing. As they slowly segue to some of the disastrous and even lethal consequences of taking the drug if you have one or another conditions, the lady on the swing is now having a walk with her friends in the park or having a barbeque.

What is the intention in the latter part of the advertisement where the positive images are stepped up? Nothing to worry about? Look how happy this beautiful young lady is!

In fact maybe the drug is good for certain people and bad for others. But isn't the imaging trying to tell you how great a lifestyle you could have if you only took the drug?

In this case, the narrative could be no, never. I will never endanger myself like that. Or it could be, "I am not sure this is applicable to me? Sounds dangerous! I better ask my doctor." Or it could be, "Wow! I hate my life. These symptoms are making me miserable. I hope my doctor will let me have it."

None of these narratives are necessarily thought out and hence they are instinctive and not reflective. However, if someone knew about their symptoms and vulnerabilities and the dangers of the drugs, and after analysis, said yes or no, it could be reflective. The NO then is something that could be respected, even if the analysis, for one reason or another, is flawed, owing to an absence of correct information or a misinterpretation of some of the words of the ad.

· · · · ·

What do you think of pharmaceutical ads that show friendly, happy interacting people but talk about horrible symptoms, even death, if you take their drug? Is there a shift in your feelings when they start to dig into the symptoms of the disease, particularly if you have symptom potentially affected by the drug and its so-called pain-relieving benefits? When you watch one of these advertorial scenarios, how do you feel during its broadcast? Is there a further shift when presented with the dangerous, sometimes even fatal side effects of the drug? Do you ever run off to your doctor to get prescribed, or start out feeling that way, and then change your mind? Do you think the images help offset the sense of danger when the side effects are explained?

• • • • •

You Can't Keep Big Pharma Down!
-Pandora's Box is a TV Set. And That's the Kind of Box
They Want Live In! It Must Not Be Abandoned!

The pharmaceutical industry is enormously successful, and much of its success is generated by ads, as well as its close affiliations with doctors, hospitals, and medical schools. If you look at the kind of advertising they do, you can see the immense and, I guess, generally successful- efforts and money they put into advertising on television.

Recently they HAD slightly backed off their advertising, but now they're back with a vengeance in 2021.

According to a Washington Post workblog written by Jason Millman and posted back on March 23rd, 2015, "It's true: Drug companies are bombarding your TV with more ads than ever," dropping back might have been a big mistake. He notes that the United States "is just one of a few countries that allows drug companies to advertise directly to patients." The article says:

> Maybe you've noticed that prescription drug ads are everywhere these days — more so than usual. You wouldn't be wrong. It was just a few years ago that TV advertisements of prescription drugs had dropped off by twenty percent, as drugmakers were also cutting back on other types of direct-to-consumer advertising. Those days are over, though, according to figures provided by Kantar Media, a market research firm. Drugmakers in 2014 spent $4.5 billion marketing prescription drugs, up from $3.5 billion in 2012. That's also up from the $2.5 billion drugmakers spent in 2000,

or $3.39 billion in 2015 dollars when adjusted for inflation.[1]

The article further points out that "direct-to consumer ads" are just a tiny bit of the money spent on soliciting health providers. In 2012 the author notes when consumer marketing had leveled out at $3.5 billion, Big Pharma spent $24 billion trying to reach the doctors.

Look, I love doctors and I love the possibilities for medical science. If you look at what has been accomplished in the medical field, it is outstanding.

But as I have indicated, science is a two-edged sword, bringing us television and mobile phones but also the possibility of total annihilation through nuclear weapons and millions of fatalities due to the deterioration of the environment, as in pollution of our water and air.

The vastness of Big Pharma's advertising is mind-boggling, but you only have to tune into television to notice it every few minutes.

High Alert

As sales practitioners, we must always be on "high alert" in regards to the word no. For this reason, we shall examine how and why a sensitivity to the hearing and saying of the word no can have a tremendous impact on the sales process. We shall look at it from the standpoint of cognitive science and narrative theory and learn how a bit of self-examination and willingness to change can radically alter the profitability of the sales process in favor of the sales practitioner- without impacting negatively on the value of the process for the client.

No and Authority Figures

What is your narrative when it comes to authority figures? Your boss is someone to sell your ideas to. How about public authority? Recently when thinking about a forthcoming interviewer with a home owner in my city, I suddenly woke up to the fact I was absent-mindedly driving 50-mph in a 35-mph zone.

Before the police officer even had a chance to engage her flashing lights, I had pulled over and rolled down my window. Why would I harm others and myself by speeding and day dreaming behind the wheel just to save sixty seconds of road time? I'm thankful for help and guidelines.

Furthermore I enjoy that I live in a community where someone else has determined safe road values. When I feel challenged by those guidelines, I attend our democratic opportunities shaped by neighborhood, city, and county public forums where I have regularly participated. But I don't challenge an individual employed to protect me, my livelihood, and others.

Do you think this homeowner/police officer understood my ability to receive NO speeding in the context it is meant? To save lives? You bet. This was a time to take a very personal correction and make a good impression.

A Look at Higher Authority

Although we are very concerned about conforming to legitimate authority that respects the rules of law designed to protect the community and further its decency and wellness, we need also to be concerned that the rules that are being dealt with are legitimate, and if they are, that authority is enforcing them and not their own rules. I believe the framework for creating responsible laws conforms to the spiritual value expressed in the injunction to "Love thy neighbor as thyself." This injunction, expressed in many different ways, is in my opinion a direct expression of connection to a Higher Power, which has, as the Declaration says, "has endowed us with certain alienable rights" but also certain inalienable responsibilities, all based on this very simple idea of loving your neighbor but also implicitly yourself.

Although shortly we are going to get more deeply into cognitive science and the narratives, which often control us unconsciously, I just want to point out that the source of real wisdom is the deep connection within ourselves, which ties our own sense of ourselves to Higher Power.

In the New Testament, and I speak here somewhat simplistically, the word soul, as in various translations, refers to the component of individuality within ourselves, roughly our personality. On the other hand, the word spirit refers to that aspect of ourself, which is tied directly to the Creator. This same distinction can be found in various psychological and spiritual belief systems.

BACK TO NEUROPHYSIOLOGY

No matter how much neurophysiology can guide us, and I do believe it can be of great value, our sense of ourselves and our decision-making ways is tied to our spirits, which is a connection that has survived before and will survive after the many accounts and theories of man's connection to his brain. That connection links us directly to narratives within ourselves that are wholly good, wise, and nurturing, and when properly discerned, are worthy of our obedience and service.

Nonetheless we human beings need a wide variety of help, and sometimes this kind of science is also a gift from Higher Authority. So in that spirit, let us return to the neuroscience we feel we can help us.

First, a bit of jargon.

In this book, we will use the word frame quite a bit. We will use a definition from *A Glossary of Cognitive Linguistics* by Vyvyan Evans:

> Frame: A schematization of experience a knowledge structure, which is represented at the conceptual level and held in long-term memory and which relates elements and entities associated with a particular culturally embedded scene, situation, or event from human experience. Frames include different

sorts of knowledge, including attributes and relations between attributes.2

When we are in the middle of a sales process, we could say we
are in a frame called "sales process," which will consist of a certain
structure by which we hope to engender a hearty yes, I want it,
from the client, followed by a rapid acceptance of a proposed purchase price, perhaps following a certain number of back-and-forth
negotiations.

The frame itself can contain narratives that set forth certain
details about its content that define the nature of the frame. The
effect of these narratives on the brain can be measured by different
instrumentation at time and compared to each other.

A frame in the sales process could be said to be analogous to a
frame describing learning to drive a car. All the focused, dedicated,
and repeated practice you consciously put into the learning process
of placing your hands at the ten and the two. Having already
placed the key in the ignition and foot on the gas, you shift into
drive and pull forward. Once your skill was mastered with the repeated and focused practice, it moved from the conscious mind to
the unconscious mind.

After a period of repeated thinking about your choices of
roads, stops signs, yields, and parking over two to three cycles of
twenty-one days. Your new thoughts and learning become part of
your internal perception. Driving is no longer new and nerve rack-
ing. You can turn on the radio and sing along. You can then more
easily understand how I could absent-mindedly drive too fast in a
very familiar neighborhood.

What is a frame in cognitive science? What is a narrative? How are frames related to narratives? How can they be used to explain inexplicable behavior? Why are narratives useful to know about in practitioner/client relations? Although this knowledge of narratives is helpful, in what sense is it limited?

The Sacred Art of Questioning

One of the most important little gems of wisdom I have uncovered in my life is so common that it could almost be said to be a cliché. And it applies not only to your relationship to the people and world around you but also to God.

Even though it is commonly said, I wonder sometimes how many people take it seriously and vigorously apply it to their lives. This little five-word phrase may be the secret key that the proverbial Aladdin may have used in negotiating with his lamp is none other than:

IT NEVER HURTS TO ASK

Now I said this, I hope you don't think that I am now going to expound on the mysteries of manifestation as explained in the famous video and book, *The Secret*, famously presented to the world at one point by Oprah. No, although I believe there is such a thing as manifestation, I do not wholeheartedly agree with *The Secret's* interpretation of reality. I don't know about the universe but, you know, it never hurts to ask God.

I also believe in another little phrase I once heard recited in Spanish: El hombre propose, El Dios depone: Man proposes, God disposes.

So I do think it is all right to ask God for things both big and mundane. It is a perfectly human trait.

45

But there is more to God and his universe than the simple paradigm of genii providing you with everything you might ask. As we will discuss, aligning your thoughts and desires with the Divine Will is not really part of *The Secret* paradigm, but it is to Oprah's credit that when she had some members of the video on her show, she commented (I paraphrase), I understand about the visualization techniques and affirmations, but what I did when confronted with choices about my future, I asked, God, what do You want me to do? How can I best serve You?

The fact is if God manifested so readily, there would be no sales. Everyone on Earth would just be given a lamp.

But I want to tell you that there are other sides, somewhat sacred as well, in the phrase, "It never hurts to ask."

Because questions help disclose reality, and seeking the truth about reality ("Seek the truth and the truth will set you free") is an action that I believe is very pleasing to God, especially when it is a truth that will help you serve His design, which includes being of service to other human beings.

So in our White Hat role, we know that it is the consciously articulated thought processes that generally prompts the yes or no, whether the narrative these things are based on are reflective or reflexive, or even if the agenda behind the response is mostly hidden in the client's unconscious. To be able to deal with these answers, you need to have a clue as to what those narratives are.

The royal route to discerning and understanding these narratives is through questioning. This will eliminate a lot of surprises and give you information as to why a certain point-of-view might reign.

Before any serious selling, or even beginning the presentation can commence, a sales person may engage in many questions designed to elicit information from the client to appropriately discover what purchasing options would please the client. The practitioner could also discover needs the client has that could be accommodated to in the interest of closing the deal. Although this can be done in a casual way, this questioning can accomplish a lot of preventive maintenance before the selling might begin.

As an example, imagine you are a realtor like me, engaged in questioning an older couple about their decision to find a home. After several minutes of engaging them, you might find out that they are moving out of their homes because of potential prospective changes in their upscale neighborhood. Despite the upscale nature of their neighborhood, a higher concentration of industrial/commercial area seems to be inviting adverse traffic activities, more noise, traffic congestion, and loss of valued health services. Not only does that couple express that they feel their neighborhood may fall behind in value appreciation, but there is a conspicuous escalation in crime. In fact one of their fine dining restaurants was actually robbed in the middle of the day, also, a commercial bank. Recently a local gang terrorized a public bus, making older women empty their purses.

For them they have a growing recognition that safer transportation and a stronger community infrastructure would have longer-term benefits to their lifestyle, ease of mobility, and overall wellness. They now wish to exit as quickly as possible to capture profit and move to a more social area.

Through watching them carefully and questioning them, you now know they need some kind of proof of the stability of the neighborhood they are moving into. They relate the story, but they don't relate the "need for proof." As they are now in your office and have decided to look at a specific home or condo, they have identified themselves as a couple who are ready to move.

Including their true needs in the process, the procedures of narrowing the choices based on the technical points of price, square feet, and neighborhood restrictions has resulted in their choosing eight to ten top notch opportunities. Advancing to the next step where are you getting out of your cars and you begin to point some of the charming landscaping in the front of the house and note their strange restlessness. Realizing in this fairly rare situation, the couple is more concerned with the nature of the nearby neighborhood than the house itself at this point; you invite them to take a closer at the neighborhood before progressing to the real walk-through of the home.

In regards to the first house we visit, your clients are not thrilled at the lack of easy access to city parks, main thoroughfares, and few mature trees. And then in reflection, one of them notes there are multiple homes with trucks parked on the front lawn. Yes, maybe there is still a lot of due diligence to do before they choose the right state of conditions for their home. This process helps us have a better understanding of what they don't like. We are now proceeding towards finding a dream home.

Now with the information you have acquired, more than ever you are equipped to handle the couple's concerns in the right way. They go back to their prospective home, relaxed and ready with two things. We have agreed on the timing for their adventures on locating house and create a list for them that expertly fits their criteria of neighborhoods they will drive through to emotionally and logically acclimate themselves.

· · · · ·

How much questioning do you use in approaching your client or making a presentation? Are you fine with your current approach? If not, how could you improve? Would the fact that you are searching for hidden narratives to help define their behavior and needs further refine the way you question?

· · · · ·

How to Deal with The Second Magic Word

Ever hear the expression, "A stick has two ends?" This is a wonderful concept for every sales practitioner to remember. It prevents prematurely categorizing experience. Sometimes a prolonged argument with a seemingly obnoxious stranger can turn into a lifetime friendship. An entrepreneurial effort on the brink of disaster can suddenly become the watchword of a whole industry. A TV series that you dismissed after the first fifteen minutes but previewed again can become the most engrossing, addictive TV program you have ever seen.

For instance a final big bad NO could be the outcome of a long tedious process and spell sadness, disgust, a feeling of rejection, or even anger for the industrious and hopeful sales practitioner.

But should that be the case, even if the no is pronounced with a great deal of conviction and firmness?

How you hear no has everything to do with what the word actually conveys to yourself and others.

Understanding your prospect's way of thinking is critical to creating the best possible sales process, but will your way of thinking or emotionally reacting to their responses foil your efforts?

Sometimes that NO and getting what it really means can be the lever that can turn the sale positive and triumphant.

I grew up driving trucks and lived in a farming town where so much corn grows, there are no trees for miles. When I moved from Mount Pleasant, Iowa, I grew to love people who didn't farm. I found meaning in helping them live wherever they chose.

The meaning of no, as you will soon see, can vary significantly, as that magical little word (please is not the only magic word) can carry nuances far beyond ordinary denial. Understanding what no means can truly change your attitude towards yourself and to others. And once you really penetrate its nuances, you will be able to control your effect on other people in an extraordinarily beneficial way. Believe it or not, the word no can have very affirmative meaning in a certain context, and the variability in the way you say it can produce a wide variety of distinctive outcomes. In fact if you understand it, you can almost say it is the second magic word.

When you hear a word that connotes a frame, it pops up in the unconscious realm of the listener, those parts of the brain we mentioned that is working, even if you don't remember their names. In fact it can be one or several narrations or schemas, which means sequences of events related to various terms, which could define a quick, reflexive response. This is what the sales practitioner has to look out for, a no which has an irrational, self-defeating or just plain ignorant narration standing behind it.

For instance the no could be a knee-jerk reaction to a certain price, the basis for a fast, almost angry, and definite no simply in my case, because the client is not aware of typical real estate transactions and does not even realize the possibility for negotiating a price. The home in which I grew up at 404 E. Monroe Street, Mount Pleasant, Iowa sold for the equal of some of the down payments of many homes I broker in Florida. It's all relative. Granted this does not happen all the time, but it does occur.

Overcoming Narratives Fueled by a No!

The no could be because there is a very sloppy paint job in the porch area. It could be because one of the children's rooms looks like it was hit by a grenade with a portion of a nice oak paneled floors pummeled with skid marks. If the realtor knew that would have been a serious concern, she or he could easily have told the client that the owner had already promised to fix them before the transaction was completed, but the no came a bit too soon. Still although the abruptness was a shock, the realtor did not react to the finality of the client's tone and her feeling of violation by its rudeness. Rather she remained open and calm and explained to him that it was her fault she had forgotten to explain that the owner of the house had already scheduled a remodel of that room in the next week, whether there was a sale or not. Her calmness saved the day, and the client, who surprised himself with his rudeness, apologized several times to the realtor before writing out a check for the down payment.

But what were the hidden narratives? Perhaps the realtor eventually uncovered the client's by questioning him, or perhaps she just realized that the tone of his voice and its finality, it didn't come out of the blue.

Now in terms of the client, we can imagine one possible narration to explain it (one out of thousands). It could be that when he saw the wall of the children's room, he remembered a tremendous problem he had with a house painter who suddenly left town, leaving behind a half-finished mess, which had been paid for in advance and required considerable money just to repaint certain areas. Fueled by that memory and a narrative that said, "No more of this crap in my life," he made an outburst without even asking a question about possible repair. In a burst of impatience, he had said no, even though he really liked the house and had not reflected on better ways with dealing with his painful memory.

In terms of the sales practitioner, who had just recently lost a sale because of small kitchen area with a broken stove and some nasty residue on the walls and was still angry about her treatment, the no sparked a desire to tell her new client off rather than try and convince him of everything. Her narrative, fueled by this other client's rudeness, was similar to her current client's narrative, "No more of this crap in my life..." But by calming down and ignoring her mini-outrage, she managed to quietly present a calm demeanor and a reasonable explanation. By doing this, the client was able to be talked out of his NO! So the practitioner knew.

Turning the Other Cheek

For myself, returning rude, aggressive behavior with calmness and love was a great big challenge. Yet I knew that the immediate, instinctive desire to reply in kind to bad behavior (an eye for an eye and a tooth for a tooth) is an instinctive reaction of the lower mind and is easier than putting brakes on that kind of emotion and trying to respond kindly with reflective consideration for the actual root of the problem that caused the reaction.

Yes, I am talking about what Jesus and Gandhi both taught and what formed the heart of the original American civil rights movement. Great things can happen if you can use forbearance.

Is there a time when violence must be met with defensive aggression? Yes, I am not going to stand around idly when I am attacked by some intruder in my house, and if compelled by the circumstance, I will use the mace, the judo chop, or a licensed handgun, I will use it to protect my life or the people that could be harmed by the thief.

Now obviously weaponry or karate kicks are not usually part of a sales scenario. Yet those very same scenarios can possibly include an attempt for theft or fraud on a very large scale. Then you may need the authorities.

But in general, the response to rudeness should be kindness and forbearance.

Get Your Informal Problem-Solving Degree

When you are prepared as a problem solver in your mind, then you are authentically prepared to say, "No problem." Even if you aren't enrolled in business school, the universe will eventually give you a degree.

When a fairly solvable objection pops up, the right technique, inquisitive and friendly, should bring the actual problem to the surface. Completely understanding what the problem is will help you to resolve it and allow the sale to be made.

Not-so-quick to solve problems involves a little deeper preparation. Deeper questioning, like what do we do next if this doesn't work? Understanding the price, timing, and considerations of your sales contract is your first step in understanding your process and procedures. Understanding the long-term relationships and greater pipeline of activity outcome you want is your goal to fulfill.

In sales you build mental real estate with each opportunity. Each opportunity offers you problem solving situations that lead to satisfied clients. Satisfied clients come when you have navigated a transaction process with orderly procedures and delivered what you said you would deliver.

Your brain is like a fingerprint, unique to you and storing these into your unconscious mind. The unconscious mind is where 99.9 percent of your mind activity is with its root level shared with your emotions and perceptions. What you say and do comes from your conscious mind, a component of your psyche that is impacted by everything in your unconscious mind.

You are building on their current mental process for which you find yourself an expert, it's important to understand the process bumps in the transaction road for which you need to exercise caution before you are on top of them. Learn the road. Know the map, backwards and forwards. This gives you freedom to explore the process speed in which you can travel with clients.

Everything you say and do is first a thought. Nothing happens until you first build that thought. Clients can become overwhelmed by some of the smallest setbacks based on words, actions, behaviors that had toxic implications in their past. What you bring to the table can energize the situations with the possibilities their transaction opportunity brings.

Literally energize. Our brain generates more energy in one day than all the cell phones on the planet. The Institute of HeartMath found that thinking and feeling anger, fear, and frustration caused DNA to change shape according to thoughts and feelings, reducing quality expression. They found the negative shutdown or poor quality of the DNA codes was reversed by feelings of love, joy, appreciation, and gratitude. Staying positive significantly overcomes and reverses any negativity that walks into the room in the form of another person's attitude.[3]

Because you are the expert and your client a novice, no matter how much experience they have buying or selling the product or service you represent, they don't have your daily training and attention to its detail. They don't have the mental pathways that have been built up over and over again. Reinforced. They don't have the neuroplasticity you have which is because whatever we think about the most will grow. As you relive the event and transactions of your process and procedures over and over, you are wiring them deeper into your mind. Your neurons fire close together and enable more rapid thought and decision-making.

So feed the positive solution building situations and starve the anger, fear, and frustration that frustrate your client. Be empathic. Your empathic attentiveness to possible reflexivity in the word no could be part of the problem. The sales practitioner needs not to lose their patience over a little itty bitty no, no matter how forcibly pronounced.

You wouldn't lose your patience over teaching a young person to drive their very first automobile. In fact very few would choose to teach a young person to drive in a Ferrari.

Growing up in Iowa, many of us at the tender ages below ten found ourselves on some type of vehicle helping with the farm work. Certainly no parent in our situation would ever put a pre-teen on a vehicle, which could hurt him or her. We start on something simple as our brains are not fully developed to handle the entirety of more complex operations. We are guided, guarded, and given lots of coaching.

If you come to Midwest Old Settlers and Threshers Reunion five days ending Memorial Day each year in Mount Pleasant, Iowa, you and your child will get to experience what farm life was like, including a safe obstacle course for your child to drive a tractor.

It can be difficult to be the adult learners who finds themself in a child's position of learning. Professional questioning, tone of voice, grace, and conscious listening will help you, the sale practitioner, really understand where to gain their full attention and help them pay deep, focused attention to the task you have been enlisted to help them with their transaction.

Focusing on problems as process points is like teaching someone to drive. Accessing the relative age and neuroplasticity of your client will present you with the ability to focus on your client as a unique individual. Your client is someone who has a previous experience and who wants a safe and happy trip toward the enjoyment of their product or service. Clients will shut down and walk away from strong beneficial opportunities if they personally feel treated unfairly.

Did you ever get so frustrated with learning to drive that you just put the car in park? This can happen to your client's brain. Where did you or the situation overload them?

Another dangerous practice is irrelevant, poorly-times multi-tasking. The kind of multi-tasking that leads to traffic accidents when texting, something legislators are clamping down on.

No one is going to make a citizen arrest if you are quickly texting back on your phone when talking to a client.

But there is a potential penalty. While engaged in texting or say writing down some notes not related to your conversation with a client but pretending to pay attention, you may be freezing your intake of external incoming communication from the person you are serving. Simultaneously you will be freezing your ability to respond whole-mindedly with professional acumen that moves you both towards a successful interaction. Obsessively responding to texting instead of the task at hand: observing your client's reactions, insights, and observations is more important than the beeps on your phone.

Stay focused. Every incomplete, rapid, and poor-quality shift of thought is like a Dairy Queen Blizzard in your brain, creating patterns of flightiness. Remember how you had to turn off the radio in the car the first time you learned to drive (or the adult in the car did)?

Think then when you are with a client, you ARE learning how to drive for the first time, and THEY demand your immediate attention.

Your non-focused frame of mind can keep them feeling positive with a financial exchange by rewarding your awareness and ability. This is managing the perception of the environment and managing our environment at the same time. Clients will grow mentally and grow trust. When asked they will be happy to send friends and family to you as referrals when they feel this way.

Questioning, analysis, empathy, and awareness are all part of the process of handling a no. You are the special unique ingredient to helping. You are building the nerve pathways that create this mental real estate: a nice boulevard without crazy exit and on ramps of over-flow traffic impeding your progress.

. . . . .

> How in fact do you handle rejection in general, in a sale, in getting a job, in relationships? Create your own best re-flective, conscious narrative? What would you surmise are three negative reflexive narrative that haunt you, even when you are handling everything perfectly OK despite the experience of a recent rejection?

. . . . .

You are helping your clients visit Happy Town, guiding your Cclients though Success Village. No is not a U-turn to leave. It's a yield or stop sign for safety!

The Approach

My approach to NO has its origins in real estate negotiations. Yes, my approach has been adapted from what has been proven in the world of real estate negotiations buy drawn from successful practices used effectively in every culture from every continent. So this is a cross-cultural approach, appealing to people on a human nature based level.

• • • • •

It's early one day in February of 2015, just about a month before the first time I'm penning these lines. It's a gorgeous Sunday. It's sunny. Blue skies. I'm standing by this pool.

At least ten couples are coming to the first Open House for my listing that is only six-days-old. Many gave me the opportunity to receive their NO gently and gracefully. Some simply left without saying a word, got to their car, and called their agent to write an offer on the home. If I had been impressed by all of the "negative" feedback from buyers that day and closed down early, I would have missed the opportunity to sell this home AND help the other attendees find their dream home.

3022 River Woods Drive Parrish, FL 34219
SOLD in nine days.

Let's do some math here. Ten couples. One of them bought this home. One of them bought another home the following week. One of them listed their home with me. One of them is going to buy a home through me in three months. One of them is going to buy a home through me in twelve months. That's a 50% conversion. And I'm not done converting. Thirteen days later as of tonight at 9:00 P.M., the new listing I met from this very same open house has a contract.

Since that time, I have had multiple transactions with those buyers and sellers by staying in touch weekly and monthly with community content. Choose your best methods for contacting and inviting clients to do business with you. Then double your efforts this year.

I know, it almost sounds like I have a pipeline of business. Yes, I am a realtor who sells homes at open houses. But let's not tag the way I created these conversions to my professional engagement and make the mistake of tying my seemingly successful approach only to real property. Don't make the mistake that people are different now. Nope. People have dreams, desires, and the need to fulfil them. The intensity has increased because of our stimulators. It works for any product or service, and I am going to show you how, but focus on my chosen profession for most of the examples.

> All of us who have been in sales know that there is a time to quit pressing a prospective client for a sale. We also know that sometimes phenomenal determination, persistence coupled with patience can produce fantastic results, as in my last example. Recall some of your best examples of having to make this kind of decision. What criteria do you use as to deciding whether to press on with a sale or to quit?

Speaking of open houses, I think it is as good a business metaphor for what I am writing about as any business, so will draw upon it to make my point. Let us say, in actual reality, open houses is functioning as my portal of activity and service and this is the primary condition needed for it to function. During the time allotted, the house is open for inspection from the public. At this time, anyone can come in.

The technology exists now that I used social open portals to help consumers gain access to my offerings from my home office.

I still interface and I still grow in my neighborhood expertise.

The neighborhood of whatever house is in question, and its related economic reality (the type of stores, offices, employment opportunities, amenities- entertainment, sports activities, recreational venues, etc.) will affect the nature of the current market for home ownership. The people who enter its unlocked doors will customarily dress in such a way as to reflect their place in the social and economic environment in which they currently live and hope to retain through their purchase in this new neighborhood. Their dress reflects the fruits of their labor, and this is relative to the neighborhood they have journeyed from and their social and economic status. In my typical open house, we are talking about rather well-paying positions, including CEOs, CFOs, active and retired military.

The open house is a stage for my sales activities. The open portal creates that one of many opportunities to meet clients who have identified themselves as willing and able to make a move.

The curtain opens when the designated time and place for guests to arrive in the auditorium officially begins. Until this time, the actor, as Stanislavski says, must prepare!

> Yes, much of my key sales involve an open house as my main stage for sales presentations. Now there are many different ways of selling, but for me, the hands-on way, with the house right there in front of the client to explore and inspect, is the right choice. As a sales person, what kind of choices to you have for your "stage" within the various options for selling. Have you evaluated other options for your "main stage?"

The Sales Practitioner on Stage

I want to use "acting," as in film and on the stage, as analogous to certain behavior involved in sales. In fact I would like to asset that ACTING IS AN ESSENTIAL COMPONENT OF THE SALES EXPERIENCE.

Clearly choosing a metaphor for "acting" could be misunderstood. It might seem "inauthentic"-like, as an old song says, "Putting on the agony, putting on the style." Well, no metaphor is entirely perfect, but let me defend this one for a moment.

What you do in sales is indeed scripted. Not scripted in a rigid word-for-word way as some films and stage plays are but in the sense of containing content that must be presented. Even in improvisational comedy, there is often a general idea of the direction of the performance, and in some films, under certain directors, there is a script to be followed, but the director intentionally allows improvisation and indeed improvisation, deviation from the projected path (but not its overall trajectory) can make for some outstanding performance.

Yes, by "acting in sales," I mean, no matter what you are selling, there is a certain ideational ground that has to be covered. For instance, in the open house, there is a house for sale and there is a stated price, which may be flexible, but it is stated nonetheless. There are details about the house, which are advertised, but an open house is also showtime, and therefore these elements are often shown and discussed, but also other caveats, benefits, and amenities will be covered not in any published advertisement.

Now in the actual theater, including films, there have been lots of theories and methodologies of acting floating around, and every director has his own point of view.

There are some stage experiences that are entirely "staged," which means there is a script to be read, memorized, and interpreted by the actor, and nothing else is to be done, except to perfectly follow the stage directions the director has chosen, step by step, exactly as he says to.

But there is another type of acting, sometimes used in theater and film, which goes to the other extreme. In its almost purest form, it is found in improvisational theater, particularly in groups, which do improvisational comedy, in which there is no script, just rough guidelines.

In selling you can also have a variety of choices as to following an exact script for a sales presentation, where there is little or no interaction between yourself and your "audience" until it is over with. And then there is the person who never gives a formal presentation but starts the sales meeting in a casual way and builds his or her case through an interaction that may focus on, yes, indeed asking questions of the proposed buyer.

This improvisational, conversational method is generally what I use in an open house. But I guarantee you, in my mind, I have a comprehensive checklist of everything I am going to cover-up to and including negotiations with the client and any ensuing paperwork.

For this type of "performance" at the open house, I usually do what students of what the legendary Russian director Stanislavski were taught to do. I prepare. In fact one of his classic books is called *An Actor Prepares*, and to his readers, he gives very good advice.[4]

One of the things actors who follow the "Stanislavski Method" do is to learn how to relax. Before they can enter into the concentrated and focused state they need, they must escape from the tensions arising from the day-to-day cares and worries that all human beings face. You could say at this point, I try to emulate those actors and I relax and focus, so I can put my thinking cap on and prepare for the actual performance.

The Actor Prepares, the Curtain Opens

At this point, before the open house begins, I might go over the specific points I may need to bring up for my guests. Undoubtedly no matter how high my conversion of presentations to sales, I am going to hear a bunch of NOs and sometimes to say a bunch when the proposed buyer puts forth a ludicrous but extremely well-wished for affordable price or insists on certain impossible changes to the structure of the house, which would mean the seller would have to unfairly put out thousands of dollars before the sale for a perfectly good house.

Even now, as seasoned as I am about applying my understanding of The Right Way to Say or Hear NO! Platform, I could conceivably cave in to my automatic, unconscious side and be quite ungracious when I hear some of the dumbest objections, ridiculous offers, and rudest interchanges that anyone could imagine. I must steel myself against this. So I say to myself, "Focus, Sandra, and don't forget! I am able to hear a NO and say a NO as gently and as gracefully as possible. It doesn't matter what they say or how they say it, you will retain your cool, kind, and responsive demeanor."

Something like that. Not a formal script but that kind of self-talk. At this point, the actor prepares (which is the title of one Stanislavski's most famous books, *The Actor Prepares*).

> Do you make any special efforts to relax and collect yourself before a sales presentation? Do you approach it like a type of theater? Do you believe your current method of sales presentations need improvement?

Being able to hear NO gently and gracefully leaves my counterpart with a feeling of having been treated with respect. It also leaves me with the opportunity to say NO. Hearing and saying NO in a well-designed and even elegant manner has enhanced my career, my value, my "brand," and my profitability. It distinguishes me from the crowd of semi-conscious realtors who have not taken upon themselves to ferret out the true foundations of a profitable and nurturing sales experience.

A sales experience of this type is always going to be largely improvisational, although elements of it could be memorized. It is going to be based on a very mindful, careful interaction with the possible buyer, an interaction predicated on your willingness, as the salesperson, to clean up your act. By this I mean the willingness to limit the most common things you're doing that hurt you in any networking opportunity. One of the main areas of concern is how you hear or say NO.

Let me go into this a bit more. When the sale practitioners hears a NO from a particular buyer (especially with an exclamation point!), it is common for the them to slip into a mild or even catastrophic sense of depression. It is like being turned down for a job you really want, a political position you have worked for months or even years, getting a rejection slip from a publisher, and in the case of real estate, losing thousands of prospective dollars in a split second.

Of course another possibility is to slip into a state of anger, and this alternative negative emotional state can lead to even worse consequences.

It is these emotional states of anger or depression, which need to be avoided at all costs. You must be steeled against any kind of interaction of that nature. Why? Because it will affect your performance immediately following the NO but also maybe for the rest of the day.

Now let me say for sure, up front, this is not an easy thing. We are not talking here about simply repressing the anger or depression, although frankly there are times when you may feel such things that you had better not say anything, even if you have to run and find a closet to hide in before that wave of anger or depression passes.

In fact we are talking about a different way of looking at people and situations that means that instead of feeling anger and depression, you feel a connection to the Divine Source within me that is miles and miles above these feelings.

But like I say, this is not an easy thing. And it is not something you can get from any one book or "system." In fact ultimately everything we learn and can trust is going to fundamentally come from within yourself.

> Although our system gives some hints as to how to change your attitude about anger, depression, and other negative emotions, we also say that our system does not pretend to provide all the answers that you might need as there are highly personal psychological, spiritual, and even technical knowledge that may be needed to fit your situation. And sometimes the most important clues can be found through your own analysis and search within. Do you think you need to work on these types of issues? What steps do you need to take to do this?

Still despite the long road we all need to traverse to perfection, the whole key to immediate sales is based on your ability to interact positively and in a nurturing way to your prospects.

Liberty, Conscience, and Connecting With People

Tolerance for other people, even their foibles, their illogical thinking, their inflammatory emotions, their inability to empathize, is a great virtue in the sales business. When we open the door or the door opens for us, we don't know who will be there on the other side. Therefore we must be ready.

What is a profitable demeanor in sales is also a profitable demeanor in life.

As I have mentioned, I personally like to present ideas about sales training in light of a job hunt and its various phases. Why? Because everyone and his brother (or sister) has to deal with getting a job, and this sometimes majorly stress-generating experience is really one of the most important sales jobs anyone will have.

<u>And the way this is best done is highly personal and involves all the techniques I am explaining in this book. And in job hunting and in interactive sales, the nature of the connection with other people is paramount.</u>

For instance 56% of those Granovetter talked to in his 1974 study, "Getting a Job," found it through a personal connection.[5] Personal connection goes beyond saying hi at an open house for a realtor. Personal connection goes beyond saying hi to your son's teacher at school or in the checkout line. Personal interactions mean going on a journey where questions are asked that create better connections. How can you do this when you feel like going into one of the empty bedrooms and crying your eyes out, or slamming your fist against one of those newly painted walls on the side of the foyer?

Not a good idea.

As your guests wander in, the first thing they will look at is that splintered plaster and that big hole in the wall. And you can bet you don't have the time to call a handyman or a painter in the middle of an open house. And believe me, it looks tacky.

One of the first rights to be protected in early America was the right of conscience, the right to believe differently on issues of religious faith. As John Quincy Adams explained, this right was a product of Christianity, "Jesus Christ…came to teach and not to compel. His law was a Law of Liberty. He left the human mind and human action free." [1]

Early American legal writer Stephen Cowell (1800-1872) agreed, "Nonconformity, dissent, free inquiry, individual conviction, mental independence, are forever consecrated by the religion of the New Testament. [2]"

President Franklin D. Roosevelt likewise declared, "We want to do it the voluntary way – and most human beings in all the world want to do it the voluntary way. We do not want to have the way imposed… That would not follow in the footsteps of Christ. [3]"

Franklin D. Roosevelt, Stephen Cowell, and John Quincy Adams in America, three generations write that if your goods aren't selling, it's probably your own fault. No one will make you believe anything here. And no one is going to be forced to believe something they don't want here.

If You Don't Deliver…

If you talk a good talk but don't deliver, soon we will figure it out. No one's buying.

You can think and do and go however and whenever you want. That's fine. But what do others think about your product. Not what do you think. So how are you helping others find your product? Are you really making it available? Do others need your product, and is it perceived as being more valuable and/or scarcer than their current choices?

> **How much responsibility do you take for your sale results? How much responsibility do you take for everything that happens to you in life?**

You really do need a combination of clarity, acuteness of vision and foresight to really succeed in a big way. You also need hammer strength.

Men and women have this in different ways.

If men had to wax their chests as often as we wax our eyebrows, the hospital emergency room would be too full to fit car accident victims in.

But still despite my current applications of my principles in my own world, my husband and my brother both have demonstrated cool, calm, collected communication in dangerous settings where I would never venture. Their remarkable careers have enabled them to translate amazing collaboration talents into successful business enterprises.

June 27th, 1996, my good friend Susie Stadnik and I strolled up to the Washington D.C. FBI headquarters and presented our dressed-up selves at the door for a very exciting reception. Joining Louis Joseph Freeh, who served as the fifth Director of the Federal Bureau of Investigation from September 1993 to June 2001, my family from around the country, we celebrated my brother's Excellence in Law Enforcement Award from The US Attorney General. The following Awards Ceremony at 2:00 P.M. in The Andrew W. Mellon Auditorium recognized he and partner John J. Liguori for working tirelessly in stopping (The First) World Trade Bombers resulting in arrest and conviction of ten individuals for acts of terrorism in the New York metropolitan area.

U.S. Department of Justice
Washington, D.C. 20530

The Attorney General's 44th Annual Awards Ceremony

Liguori   *Voss*

John J. Liguori
Christopher T. Voss
Special Agents
New York Division
Federal Bureau of Investigation

Presented to Special Agents John J. Liguori and Christopher T. Voss for their professionalism, investigative skills and interpersonal and communication skills in working tirelessly for two and one half years in investigating the case and assisting prosecutors in the TERRSTOP (World Trade Center Bombing) Trial, resulting in the arrest and conviction of 10 individuals for various acts of terrorism and planned terrorist acts in the New York metropolitan area.

His perseverance has not changed. Chris hasn't stopped. You can find him on the news, in the classroom, and in his book promoting an understanding of negotiation. The most dangerous of which is the one you don't know you are in. And so we NOW understand about the SECOND World Trade Bombers and other acts of terror.

In similar heroic fashion, my husband Mark LaFlamme flew the first night low level combat mission in B52 history, which was performed during Operation Desert Storm by three crews, receiving the Distinguished Flying Cross.

He continues to use his skills and ability to press beyond the norm and serve his clients as a Wealth Manager and co-founder of National PTSD Service Association.

I have watched their strength, tenacity, and wisdom develop over the years and watch them rewarded in the marketplace. As I have witnessed their mental resolve and strength produce measurable results, I have changed. Maybe not as much as I wish to, but I am on my way.

I know they are right in their tenacity. And by admiring and admitting that they are right, I am attempting to study and assume their exact patterned thinking skill set to become a better salesperson. A stronger business based on solid mindset and specific direction.

Yes, women want to be understood. Every talk show exemplifies the entertainment value of women who lose it on camera, as if it means their emotions are more valuable than mine. Men, on the other hand, want to be heard. They do not necessarily go as far as demanding to be understood. Blah, blah, blah, blah. I do not care if you are a woman or a very expressive man. What problem are you solving by overly expressing your emotions?

Frankly giving way to uncontrolled emotions does not impress me nor would it impress any of my friends, who like me, grew up on the farm with live animals. It is impossible to be emotional when you are saving a mare's legs from a wired fence that is about to shred the animal. Why, because if you are freaked out, the animal will freak out.

I vividly remember the first time this happened to me. I was twelve and totally alone. But seeing the pain the animal was in and the dangers if it were going to try and extract itself, I decided to intervene. At the time, I was completely aware that no matter what I did, I had to avoid its dangerous, floundering hooves, that is if I wanted to live through my rescue attempt. After rapidly composing my action plan, I approached with the rapid speed and care the event needed. In other words, I evaluated the situation, made a plan for calculated care, and acted with urgency and caution.

The result was that I freed the animal. My emotional aftermath was a combination of letting go of the fear for the animal and myself, a sense of exhilaration and sheer happiness at my success at setting her free.

Wrights Cindy, I am riding shown on the cover is the horse's name was a beautiful, loving animal who gave me lots of winning arena and field experiences for years to come after this. She was so sweet. Hours and hours of riding brought therapeutic rewiring to my ability to think, react, coordinate, and function after the head injury in the Colorado pool.

In life it's the same. People also judge by our actions and respond with enduring support. And too often, we only judge ourselves by our intentions and not our actions.

The benefit my family gave me in riding and showing Wrights Cindy was also to place me in an arena to be judged. The judge literally stands in the middle and watches your every move in every possible direction.

How do you know what to improve if you don't place yourself in the competition? I had learned the year before I won second place. Twelve months later and hours and hours of training, riding, barn cleaning, preparation at 5 A.M. and 5 P.M. paid off.

The real win was the beginning of the end-of-mayhem created by the trauma. I had a focus and mission. I had a benchmark for success. I had a community of support.

So if I had just stood there with warm intentions but watched Wrights Cindy struggle until the barbed wire slit her throat. I would have had a horrible animal horror story forever in my mind instead of a childhood happiness that launched my ability to believe I achieve great things.

END NOTES

1. Jason Millman, "It's true: Drug companies are bombarding your TV with more ads than ever." *Washington Post Workblog, March 23, 2015*

    http://www.washingtonpost.com/blogs/wonkblog/wp/2015/03/2 3/yes-drug-companies-are-bombarding-your-tv-with-more-ads-than-ever/

2. Vyvyan Evans, *A Glossary of Cognitive Linguistic*s (Edinborough: Edinborough University Press, 2007), p.95 http://www.vyve-vans.net/GLOSSARY.pdf

3. "You Can Change your DNA," HeartMathInstitute, July 14, 2011
    https://www.heartmath.org/articles-of-the-heart/personal-devel-opment/you-can-change-your-dna/

4. Constantine Stanislavski, *An Actor Prepares*, (New York: Routledge, 1964)

5. Mark S. Granovetter, "Getting a Job," (Chicago: University of Chicago Press, 1974, 1995)

Chapter 4

YOU ARE DEFINED
BY
HOW AND WHAT YOU SELL

There is no question that in most sales encounters, even if they are beginning with business networking experiences, the bottom line is that most of the relationship, at least for quite some time, will be revolving around your product and how you handle it.

Like it or not, you are perceived by others by how you handle it. What you bring to the table is your knowledge of your product and the unique insight and understanding to solving others' problems. How you conduct yourself as a problem solver demonstrates what others may pay you. What you understand and convey about your ability needs to align with your product and the very real needs of others.

When my parents converted their gas stations to convenience stores, they sold convenience instead of just gas. I have noticed that consumers still pay for convenience. If it is a product that becomes easy to use based on prior knowledge, then it is more readily adaptable.

When there is a shift in the market or there is a new invention, there is always a shift in opportunity. And what separates us from machines is our ability to synthesize a complex never-before situation.

Yes, every bit of your relationship with the client initially will be based on what is being sold and how you are transacting the deal. Of course spiritually you will work out your own relationship with God and act accordingly. But on an intellectual and emotional level, yes, you will be defined by how and what you sell.

· · · · ·

Are you a bit uncomfortable when I say you are defined by how and what you sell? And why shouldn't you? We are not commodities. We are human beings. How do you feel about how you have been defined in the sales process? And is there anything you can do, as a rule, to overcome being judged solely on your sales-oriented behavior?

· · · · ·

Choosing Your Product

There are going to be a wide range of readers of this book. Some will be seasoned sales, veterans sick and tired of sales practices that they have used for years, probably mostly because they haven't really opened the golden door of opportunity for them that they believed initially would soon happen shortly after embarking on their career. Some of these will be seeking some kind of alternative to their sales protocol mainly because their conscience hurts, either because of the product or because of the way they are selling them.

So for some, this book will be a bit of a rescue operation.

Yes, maybe my point here is a bit controversial. But I am not about to apologize for bringing someone back to their conscience, however uncomfortable it may be for them.

When a person is brought back to their conscience, you are bringing them back to themselves.

And despite the pangs of conscience, it is better to be yourself than trapped in the false ideas of one's lower personality.

Although we will be devoting a whole chapter to hypnotic selling, the deception involved in sales practices is extensive, goes way beyond hypnosis and ranges from simple trickery to massive and unrestrained thievery.

Here's one sales practice I recently encountered.

"FREE"
HOW SOME GET RICH BY MAKING THIS PITCH

It involved the offer for an almost magical sounding investment opportunity into learning how to identify and clock into the exact, best moment to invest in a certain commodity. The great thing about the chance to get very detailed information is that it would be free and would be found in a book that would be dispensed to the prospective client after watching a relatively short video (well, maybe not so short).

But the reality was, and it is not always the case with this type of marketing scenario, that the book *was* free, but only if you bought the subscription. And in my mind, this clearly wasn't the implication of the pitch to get the book. *Free* meant *free*?

• • • • •

Can you peacefully live with yourself regularly engaging in that kind of marketing? How do you feel when you experience a "bait and switch" sales trick, even if you are not really hurt? Have you ever been involved in anything like this, as either a consumer or a sales person?

.   .   .   .   .

Current neuroscientific and quantum physics research confirms that our thoughts change our brains daily.

When we are involved with distorting the truth, we are wiring this perverseness into our brains, and in a sense, creating brain damage.

We are not merely pointing to the community harm done with sales trickery. We are also noting the work done by the neurological community, which is documenting that learned fear creates chaos and havoc in our brains to such a degree that is measurable decrease in activity in the lateral prefrontal cortex (just above your temples). This is the area in the brain where the neurological circuits would normally have generated and maintained strategy, a core feature of human intelligence, mapping out future behavior by considering numerous complex variables.

You will shorten your ability and brain function by employing distortion. Not a happy consequence for bad, deceptive behavior.

> Have you ever seen unexpected consequences occur from a sales or similar negotiation following some kind of smaller, perhaps a seemingly insignificant warning sign of the possible dishonesty of your salesperson or associate? How should you act when you find yourself the victim or potential victim of a "bait and switch" tactic?

Whether or not the financial newsletter we have been speaking of has a righteous and profitable strategy for the investor, the little, or even big, scam is dwarfed by billions and billions of dollars spent on deceiving the public in general in a richly, diversified variety of ways. Let's examine what we can do about it.

Events and circumstances from TV and our environment enter into our minds and brains through electromagnetic and quantum worlds. We cannot control the events and circumstances of our lives, but we can control our reactions.

Our five senses activate an emotional response almost immediately, but if we don't take the time to process them, the unprocessed emotion will dominate.

By examining how the emotion causes you to act, you can examine the possible end results. If you are responding to fear, you will be producing negative results and behaviors.

Let's get some issues out on the table and decrease their level of impact on our daily lives. By discussing what we CAN do, or what our part is to play, we can also develop the courage to change. If we cannot make the change happen ourselves, we cannot at least become statesmen promoting a solution and contribute our efforts in productive directions with others to promote the change we seek...

How Corrupted is the Marketplace?

That is hard to tell.

Recently the Department of Consumer Affairs (DCA) has targeted a major "heath food" chain with intentionally "overstating the weights of pre-packaged products, including meats, dairy, and meat products." The article describing this possibly robust infraction said:

> The DCA tested eighty different pre-packaged products and found that all of them had mislabeled weights. On top of that, eighty-nine percent of the packages tested didn't meet the federal standard for the maximum amount that an individual package can deviate from its actual weight, as set by the U.S. Department of Commerce. The overcharges ranged

from $0.80 for a package of pecan panko to nearly
$15 more for a package of coconut shrimp.[1]

Characterized by the DCA Commissioner as "the worst case of mis-labeling" ever seen by her inspectors," many other stores at that time were said to being investigated by the DCA for the same type of infraction.

There are salespeople selling these packages to consumers every day. Do they know they are overpricing?

Whether the salespeople are responsible or not, or even whether the charges are true or not, it is not difficult to see that these and many other types of practices in marketing and sales are far too numerous and complex to track, much less really investigate and prosecute.

> **Given the nature of bureaucracy and the size of this type of commercial corruption, we must ask ourselves if this is a problem that can truly sufficiently addressed by government?**

Going Against the Grain

Right now the White Hat philosophy goes against the grain of much commerce. Indeed there are billions and billions of dollars that are being made in our country and in a global economy that is driven by the darkest, most exploitative thinking, a kind of thinking that has hovered around the periphery of American culture for a long, long time.

Perhaps the most dangerous thing about it, it has totally contaminated our political life, where people are saying and doing the opposite of what they are communicating to voters.

I realize that there are people reading these words who have always acted by integrity. And perhaps they believe that we are still living with the same ideals that the Founding Fathers had in mind. Isn't that what is being taught in school and often being promoted by major media?

There are various problems with honesty, believe it or not.

One of the major problems is that a person truly brought up to be honest when they are children and surrounded by meticulously honest people when they grow up, can truly lose out when they try to understand the adult world of commerce or politics because they lack the empathy needed to interpret the heart and soul of wrongdoers.

Also, the impulse to be honest has its limitations. You can still make dangerous mistakes. For instance you may be a totally honest sales person but accidentally sell a customer the wrong oil for his vehicle because you didn't bother to check or perhaps only understood viscerally or not fully prepped as you needed to be.

Besides good intentions, you also need to realize that by making you more aware and enhancing your ability to empathize with your client, to spot their or your hidden narratives, to ruthlessly expand your product knowledge, to learn when to act with boldness when you might risk the sale to truly help your client, your ability to act effectively will transcend the clear value of simple honesty. People with basic integrity will now become empowered to act with the kind of competency that is only possible when you have effectively enhanced your ability to act with full awareness in the present moment. That way you can become even more honest because you know and understand more to become honest about.

Show up when you say you will show up. Be on time. Do what you say you are going to do. Do it with excellence. Follow-up to make sure everything is working the way it was when you left. If you sell landscaping, have a beautiful yard. If you sell teeth straightening, have a gorgeous smile.

Yes, we still live in a culture whose members often define success as winning at all costs. This is a pure Machiavellian concept, but it is not confined to politics but also to commerce, business, and to personal life. And this is a philosophy and strategy we much fight against in ourselves and in the culture we live in.

In terms of products and services, the deceptive approach has had many consequences. It is an approach that has led to multiple deaths because of hidden, improperly revealed dangers in pharmaceutical products; death and injuries as a result of delayed recalls by automobile companies that knew defects existed in their cars, thousands of home clients each year facing injury and illness because of defects in a house they bought that had dangerous structural defects, black mold, asbestos, or other undisclosed defects.

All this deception involves money basically stolen by sales practitioners who knew their product didn't work as promoted and acquired sales often through deceptive testimonials. Today food is often sold with unspecified characteristics, some genetically modified without this fact being disclosed; some containing ineffectively tested hormonal constituents, pesticides, and antibiotic residues. Often this is not only a failure of vendors but also a failure of government to provide proper oversight, and I do not mean meaningless over-reaching regulation.

And so our commercial and regulatory culture sanctions small lies about what is really in a can of soup to huge lies concerning the safety of products that could conceivably cause great injury or sudden death.

At any level, being involved with enabling a shifty sale or a shocking crime affects your brain. Guess what? Massively different degrees of harm have been done with faulty packaging and faulty ethics but equally divisive to brain health.

Of course our brain health upon learning of the perpetration is impacted with various degrees of shock based on previous experience. We can educate ourselves to avoid future traps.

The brain health of the perpetrators is clearly affected by creating such a strategy.

It boils down to personal integrity, over which we can extend personal control. If such control is not exercised, then chaos, negativity, and rehearsing negative events disconnect and desynchronize the neurons in the brain. They stop firing together and no longer wire together.

In fact the result can be debilitating. Perhaps somewhat like the effect on the brain by waterboarding or having to listen to loud music twenty-four hours a day with bright light turned on. Damaging the brain will damage health and longevity. So on the most basic level, don't waterboard yourself over money or notoriety.

On the farthest end of the scale, if your trade is illegal and uses fear as your most predominate mechanism to close the deal, you are already aware of your shortened life span. Change and find a positive trade – your skill sets are transferable.

We can't change the past. We can change our present behavior. Make restitution and amends if possible. Free your mind of uneasiness. Put the past in its rightful place and leave it there.

> **Does the level of deception and outright dishonesty in our culture ever seem surrealistic, like you have arrived and lived on a planet you never even suspected when you were a child or a young adolescent? Does it make you feel helpless, or does it challenge you to make a more profound contribution, despite the obstacles?**

In the broadest sense, all these issues I have addressed are based on persons, companies, and even associations that have "sold" their integrity and trustworthiness to the public and then proceeded to either directly misinform or intentionally hide from the public key information. It is a process that requires someone "buying" into the "sale" and acting in such a way that the "product" or "service" is bought, even if we are talking about a vote or the response to a political survey. The results of the voter or consumer may then support the action, whether it is easy to discern the consequences or not.

Voters fill ballot boxes with choices marked on pieces of paper or enter them on computers. Consumers vote at grocery store counters with credit card and dollar bills. These "votes" always indicate a desire to acquire something, and to that extent, indicate a kind of approval, however, somewhat forced by virtue of the scarcity of good candidates or the need to choose the most tasty and least costly foods.

If the least harmful foods could be labeled, who would you trust to label it? Look up some of those ingredients on the Internet, some you would not dare to feed your pet, so why are you eating them? Would you keep shopping at a grocery store where every bag of food you brought home had something that poisoned you?

Although the immensity of those joining us in buying something may intimidate us, those conceivable coordinated "votes" have impact and can spell the fate of a product's longevity. Since we vote our dollars during an exchange, shouldn't the buyer have a sense of that responsibility in terms of what he wants to "say" when he buys something? Let's just continue to grow and learn how much, as consumers, our vote counts everywhere we go and in everything we do. And when we are in the role of sales practitioners, and we are directly facing those who will vote on our project, must we now be extremely sensitive to our buyer's power and utilize our sales power with sensitivity and finesse?

And now that we are writing about the changes in the market and changes in opportunities, can you see how much opportunity is available when adjustment occurs? Consumers cannot keep moving in a negative direction and thrive. Our brain does not function in that capacity for any length of time. Longevity requires positive action. Focusing on those practitioners who clearly do not care about the value of their product but concentrate entirely on how to get their money from the buyer, we would identify their practices, often involving intentional deception, Black Hat Selling.

Not every type of selling involves just black and white selling, and yes, these elements can be mixed. But further there are gray lines in some of these activities. For instance in promoting a product that is still being tested, sometimes information that is suspected but not proven might be withheld, a matter of non-disclosure to be defined by conscience and but not, at the moment, by law. Sometimes the law is ambiguous, and in Gray Hat Selling, the sales practitioner may take advantage for very moral or very immoral reasons of that ambiguity. In White Hat Marketing, the goal is to be very upfront with deeper truths, personal integrity, and to reject the practices of Black Hat Marketing.

A Reader Responds to My Real Estate Sales Blog

"But, Sandra, here in the South, people don't like being negative, so they candy coat comments in their feedback…giving homeowners the wrong impression about what their realtor is really thinking. This leads to the inaction (needed) to fix what needs fixing to get to a yes."

What a blessed comment in this real response to my blog!

Do Not Candy Coat Yourself
Maximize Trust by Speaking Straight From the Hip

There it was, a succinct but important explanation of why cloaking your true voice and the reality it wishes to offer a client can be blocked by bad cultural conditioning.

I didn't really respond to this blog because I knew I would have to say a whole lot. My response to the kind visitor is this entire book, and in particular, this chapter.

Candy coating could be-

Your house looks great, but perhaps your front porch could be touched up a bit.

When the reality is-

Your front porch needs a lot of work. Broken swings, unpainted shingles underneath the brick overlay, and an interior that has several broken beams detracts from a house that is otherwise quite well-kept. I can't sell it in that condition, except as a fixer-upper. You really need to upgrade that patio, and it will greatly increase what we can get for it.

When the owner replies-

I really can't put much energy into this now. Both my kids are out of school, and as I explained, my budget's really tight now. Can I wait?

You could say-

Well, I know how anxious you are to sell your house. So I'll put the sign up and hope for the best.

Or say something productive-

You very well may be losing thousands of dollars because of a relatively quick and easy repair. If you value the reward from the market place a buyer will give you for appealing to their desired move in ready condition, we can wait until you have the chance to fix it. I know your situation, and my job is to act in your best interest. Be confident that I work for you and will do as directed. But this isn't a huge problem. We can get it done. I know some affordable handymen and carpenters and will call them right now if you need help.

In the above scenario where I am helping with a directed, collaborative way, I am also writing. Literally. The bonding behavior shows I am attentively listening and notating what they are saying. I am also benefiting my brain. I am stimulating a collection of cells in the base of my brain known as the reticular activating systems. The RAS is the filter for all of the information my brain needs to process, and it gives more attention to what I am currently focusing. My frontal lobe is where speaking and writing are associated. This area is also responsible for movement, reasoning, judgement, planning, and problem-solving. The parietal lobe is also important in writing as it interprets words and language. Most importantly writing can have similar effects on your brain as meditation. Your breathing slows down and you get into a zone. This process and procedure will help you problem solve at the best level possible and keep a pace your client needs you to operate.

Solving problems, instead of avoiding them, builds rapport. Helping to better see the area that needs to be solved by allowing you both to see the conscious and nonconscious thought in a visual way – creating trust, understanding, and leading to a timely solution. The speed of any team moves at the pace of trust. And in a worst-case situation, documentation of agreed upon steps.

Saying NO elegantly is not always negative. It can mean:

Not now.
Not here.
Not you!

You can now help by professionally reaching out to the other professionals involved in making your transaction a success and understanding skills and abilities. The speed of this team and transaction is going to be gauged by the weakest contributing role player or the person who exhibits the least amount of information and trust.

If it's a client saying NO to you personally right now, find out why. An honest ability to hear real feedback from a valued prospect exhibits a desire to have a long-term career, creating future opportunity for collaboration. Unless something unethical happened, consumers appreciate the chance to grow and see character development.

• • • • •

> ### How do you handle cultural weaknesses in your sales activities?

• • • • •

Trustworthiness is a long-term attribute, which is rewarded over time. This trustworthiness, this adherence to high standards of fairness and effectiveness in dealing with difficult situations is exhibited by elegantly holding your ground, like realtors who helped hundreds of thousands of people move during the COVID-19 lockdown. Speaking up is only a weakness if it comes from an impure emotional stance, meaning reckless anger or contrariness, etc. Speaking out for fairness and justice is a strength and key virtue of White Hat folks in every career and job position and for every real citizen of planet Earth!

• • • • •

> ### Do you shoot from the hip, that is tell your clients what they need to know, or do you choose rather to please them, no matter what the truth is?

• • • • •

Your Competence is Defined by Product Knowledge

Let's talk about the product. Product knowledge is inextricably involved with your image.

Does it need fixing? The realtor who responded to my blog at the beginning of the chapter mentions "to fix what needs fixing to get to a yes."

Customer Disservice

Customer service is important for unforeseen issues, but I'm not a big believer in delivering goods to the market place where the marketing department already knows they are broken or flawed in some way. Or providing a customer with a multitude of invoice on, their website, in email, through a phone call, with different payment amounts for the same thing. Or you may be allowing the client to grossly undervalue the real worth of his property, perhaps due to the expediency of sales in your favor as a practitioner, or maybe you just don't want to challenge the client and you know you could sell at that price. That is what I call customer disservice.

Oh, the client or customer may not get it at first. It may take a while for the market reality to soak in. And if he or she ever gets it, then they may be shocked and angry, even if the sale price was their idea. Even a tear down home has land value. Work up from there. Be a professional. Be elegant with your NO the same way you would want to hear it.

When a homeowner says they have the nicest home on the block and they deserve twenty percent more than the other neighborhood houses, but you disagree with the assessment of the house's competitive quality, you have to think, "That doesn't work for the stock certificate of IBM. Why would it be for what *you* believe to be two relatively equal homes?"

The more personal the product is to your seller, the more elegant your NO will have to be, and the more you will have to transcend your geographic upbringing and utilize insight and understanding of your counterpart.

Will You Take That Extra Step to Prove the Value of Your Product?

Will it help them to go into comparable homes to view the competition to form a better judgment? If so, are you willing to do it? After all Burger King knows what McDonald's is doing.

So if it's real estate sales, I tell the client, "Let's all walk across the street and check this out!"

How much more elegant can that be? Like being escorted through the Ritz to the nearest rest room. In the Ritz, they don't just point you down the hallway. They take you there. In fact if you want anything, anything at all, they will make a good faith effort to get it for you. That is why the brand of the Ritz Carlton is equated with great customer service. And should you be equated with anything less? So be personable, but be ready to steel your client and yourself from any unexpected market reaction to a specific price. Often the market will be more educated than you are, so you need to keep up.

> **What extra steps can you take to personalize your sales? Do you clients truly note your extra attention, that they are not just a recipient of some kind of automated sales presentation that you have memorized, that you are awake and personally interested in their real needs?**

· · · · ·

Your Niche Market

If you are selling, you need to know your own niche marketplace quite well. What kind of buyers do you need to find and cultivate? When you do, are you equipped to deal with their specific situation?

 86

• • • • •

What is your niche market?

• • • • •

For instance when I sell a house, I also sell the neighborhood, neighbors, nearby stores, schools, parks, and other resources. And sometimes this "neighborhood selling" can be the real key to sales. It depends on the prospective purchaser. Sometimes I find I have to do a few adjustments to the house, an extra patio, fixing up the basement, some landscaping components, because the client is sold on the community but wants his home slightly customized to overcome his concerns with its limitations. Some of these things I have fixed, others I recommend.

The result is because I know my market and my marketplace so well, I have upped sales in neighborhoods, which have been very low in home sales for years. Even in neighborhoods where there have been no sales, none, I have found buyers by carefully analyzing what is the market is rewarding and exemplifying that attribute.

• • • • •

> **Write down the main aspects of product knowledge you need to know, in whatever area of sales you are involved with, that would truly give you a heads-up on whatever the client needed and allow you to offer him benefits he may not have even thought about.**

$\bullet \quad \bullet \quad \bullet \quad \bullet \quad \bullet$

To this end, be well-informed, through selectively surfing, reading relevant books, newsletters, current listings, talking to people in the neighborhood, to other realtors, to businesses, walking or riding around, getting a feel for the territory. If there are problems, are you willing to check out the options for financing, for repairs, making complaints to have things fixed that should have been previously?

Do We Dare Be Honest?
Do We Dare Disturb the Universe?

Silence is not effective if there is a bad intention obvious in a contract, a secret clause that is meant to cheat a client; if a house is toxic with asbestos and mold and the buyer has not been told, if there is some kind of sudden financial emergency that happens to the buyer, it may be the time to raise awareness with your voice, risk alienating someone or even report someone to the authorities for fraud. Speaking up, being critical, being forthright, even to the point of hurting a deal or damaging a relationship, may sometimes be necessary. Let your conscience be your guide. But let your voice be modulated by empathy, compassion, and reason, and do not swing over to the dark side of uncontrollable, supremely alienating and soul-draining anger.

Unfortunately White Hatters are not only up against competitors who perpetuate a generally deceptive and dishonest strategy to win purchases from consumers, they are up against an especially toxic sales regime, fostered by a tradition of a methodology partially based on mild trance induction but also other elements of powerful cognitive persuasion meant to nudge the buyer into reflexive thinking that fosters enhanced suggestibility.

White Hat Sales does not stand alone in wishing to offset these influences. It is built on a tradition of books that were basically consumer rights friendly and have directly or indirectly influenced the application of the sales process. Books, such as *Think and Grow Rich* by Napoleon Hill or *How to Win Friends and Influence People* by Dale Carnegie, have been influencing the same readers who have assimilated such books as Og Magdino's *The Greatest Salesman in the World,* Zig Ziglar's *Secrets of Closing the Sale,* and Kenneth Blanchard's *The One Minute Manager.*

Whereas these books and others like them may contain material that I feel are positive they are limited in their development. They are basically nurturing and aim for integrity in one's transactions and respect for the client.

• • • • •

What is the best sales system you have encountered?

• • • • •

These systems appeal to those who believe their personal progression in life and in sales must be based on honesty, that is integrity or truth, but also genuine concern for other people that is conscience. Nurturing sales systems must embody both qualities, truth and conscience.

• • • • •

How well informed are you about your product, your competitors, your sales processes? Are you up to date on what you need to know?

END NOTES

1. "Whole Foods Overcharging Customers for Pre-Packaged Foods, Department of Consumer Affairs Finds, *NBC New York*, June 24th, 2015
http://www.nbcnewyork.com/news/local/NYC-DCA-Inspects-Whole-Foods-Overcharging-Weight-Prepackaged-Foods-309593751.html

2. Spencer Ackerman, "US torture doctors could face charges after report alleges post-9/11 collusion," *The Guardian*, July 11, 2015
http://www.theguardian.com/law/2015/jul/10/us-torture-doctors-psychologists-apa-prosecution

Chapter 5

THE DARK SIDE OF SELLING
Sales Systems Designed To
Sabotage Consumer Decision-Making

We have focused on the development of a win-win sales system based on neuroscience and a type of spiritual psychology that helps separate practitioners and their clients from self-destructive semi- or unconscious narratives that block reflective decision-making.

Unfortunately some writers and marketers believe that they have an almost sacred obligation to themselves to separate their prospective customers from their money by using everything they know or can find to block the very kind of decision-making that we are trying to promote.

Would You Mind If I Very Gently Deposed You of Your Judgment, So I Could Sell You This Vacuum Cleaner?

Whereas there are techniques suggested by sales systems and books that basically follow the White Hat Path, there are also systems and books that revel in leading people closer to or tread directly on the Black Hat Path. These techniques focus on client manipulation for the benefit of principally the seller. Although these motives are often disguised by their exponents, their justification for their manipulation is basically "The seller knows best," and this gives them the right to by-pass the client's right to decision-making.

> We have made a case for protecting and supporting a client's rational decision-making. Do you support this point of view? Since nobody is looking, please explain exactly what your current point of view is on this point of view. You don't need to pull any punches.

Although, granted, many of these practices are embedded in the industry without the support of literature, the Black Hat Path has found one overwhelming approach that has been fully supported and is still intact and growing. Among other things, it embodies techniques intended to induce hypnotic trances through conversational hypnosis. It is called Neuro-Linguistic Programming (the beloved acronym is NLP), a technique first developed by Richard Bandler and John Grinder in the 1970s.

Bander and Grinder's first book was called *The Structure of Magic I: A Book about Language and Therapy*, and their second, *Frogs and Princes*, sold 270,000 books. Their work, principally developed as a kind of therapy, eventually became a platform for commercial sales.

An article called "Hypnotic Selling Techniques" by Donald J. Moine in a magazine called *Selling Power- Success Strategies for Sales Management* echoes our speculation on the widespread use of this system. In the article, the writer says:

> Back in 1981, Personal Selling Power became the first business magazine in America to feature full-length articles on the new science of Neuro-Linguis-

tic Programming (NLP) applied to sales and marketing. Many people at that time said NLP was a fad
and that it would soon be forgotten. However, NLP
has gone on to become one of the most popular new
approaches in the world to enhanced performance,
and is being used in one form or another by most
modern sales and management training programs.[1]

He further remarks that many NLP students don't realize that many
of their techniques are derived from "conversational hypnosis," a
technique pioneered by Milton Erickson, whose influence was clearly
known by Bandler and Grinder. Erickson found a way to hypnotize
people who might very well never imagined they were being induced
into a trance state.

Moine says, "This form of hypnosis has nothing to do with trick-
ing anyone or putting them to sleep. It is simply a fascinating 'mesmerizing' way of speaking."[2]

The latter is an interesting claim since in the very next sentence,
he speaks about the three characteristics of this so-called "conversational hypnosis, grabbing the listener's attention, focusing that attention and 'greatly increasing suggestibility.'"[3]

First of all, you can be put into a light trance without fully "falling
asleep."

Second of all, when someone does that to you intentionally without telling you because they use a "mesmerizing" tone, they are "trick-
ing" you to falling into an altered state of consciousness without
knowing it and without your permission. Mesmer is credited with
being a pioneer of hypnosis, although his methodology, based on the
fluidic, etheric substance, animal magnetism, was different than current practitioners who use a variety of different methods. Still the
clear connotation of the term is still "to entrance."

Thirdly, a hypnotic state can alter suggestibility. Have you ever
seen a live performance by a hypnotist who puts people in a trance

and has them do ridiculous things, like shouting loudly when a person says mister, or dancing a bit too suggestively in front of a hundred people when they are normally shy? Some of this may be faked, of course, but some of it is real phenomena but much more dangerous when it tampers with your ability to reflectively think or alters the direction of your decision-making than when it is used solely for entertainment.

> **How does this appeal to you? You are trying to buy life insurance to protect your family and somehow you slip into a state of enhanced suggestibility because of that purring mantra to buy emanating from the mouth of that slick and unconscionable NLP practitioner.**

When an author or sales trainer talks about heightening suggestibility, he or she is clearly talking about them surrendering their reflective mind to their now controlled reflexive form of thinking. The consumer has now become under the thumb of that NLP practitioner, to the extent it is possible with each individual case.

If We Mirror Them, What If They Catch On?

As an example of Moine's wondrous sales techniques, he cites one of the best ways he knows to develop trust in potential buyers.

> All of the research on trust points to the fact that we trust and like people who are like we are. The most rapid way of building trust is through the use of pacing techniques, which are matching or mirroring techniques. When you become like the other person by pacing him, you minimize and dissolve differences.

> When you are like the customer, the only way the
> customer cannot like you is by not liking himself,
> which for most people is difficult to do.[3]

To start off with, "mirroring" is not the same as being empathic or even familiar with a person's culture or background and even able to perhaps use colloquial expressions from their language or culture, which can actually be authentic and appreciated. This is deliberately feigning an identity and character that resembles your client.

Although I do talk of certain aspects of acting or playing a part to develop empathy, confidence, and the clarity of presentation, I always, always advocate projecting core authenticity. I never would want a White Hat Seller to pretend he is something he or she is not in White Hat sales, you take yourself as the necessary "baggage" in what you do. You bring your real self to the sales table. Sometimes though you may use the slang or language familiar to your client. You may use certain gestures that are not in your normal repertory. That can be, in context, just a happy way of crossing a bridge to a way of acting familiar to your customer.

If you go to a Greek wedding and they are dancing the Kalamatiano, you don't break out on a fox trot. If your Egyptian friend says, "Salaam Alaykem," you can say it back. You don't have to say hi. If you are dealing with a fifteen-year-old who likes greeting people with an elaborate handshake, and you can do it, you can follow suit if you are able to without making a fool out of yourself. It's a bonding thing.

This isn't the same as scratching one's nose ten seconds after the client scratches his and then crossing your legs right after he does. Maybe I am being unfair. Mirroring is subtler than that. You have to do it deceptively, so the client doesn't notice.

But what if he does?

> As I stated, there is a fine line between authenticity and conforming to some of the cultural and personal modes of communication of a client? How do you see this fine line? What is the role of "acting" in your sales activities? Have you heard of "mirroring" before? Have you ever used it? Do you think I am being too hard on these Black Hat marketers?

Why Not Just Throw All Hesitation to the Wind And Dynamically Brainwash Your Customers? The Salesman Knows Best! Right?

For many decades in the twentieth century, and even now in the new millennium, what are called NLP sales theories in practice involved a hodgepodge of techniques designed to create reflexive buying behavior through varying compounds of aggressive sales techniques, including frequent efforts to close sales before ending the sales presentation, investigating and mirroring conditions, which led buyer to purchase previously, using repetition, controlled intonation of key words to heighten the suggestion to buy, using rosy narratives, regardless of their validity, to garner the sale.

Whatever the original idea, here are what some people propounding to use the NLP system inform us.

On YouTube, one nice, young lady asks us to remember to repeat "*by now*, you know" during a sales script many times. Like "*by now*, you know that we have-" or "*by now*, you've probably known that." So that at the end of the sales, "closing time" you ask them if they want to "buy now" and they've heard that phonetic match, "by now," they will be more ready to buy now. A tiny little repetition based on the fact that repetition can heighten suggestibility in certain circumstances.

Her second technique is slightly darker. She recommends putting a "Buy Now" button on your sales video. The "Buy Now" button will have an inconspicuous, flickering pixel that cannot readily be seen consciously. That way as people watch the video, their minds will be unconsciously riveted on the fun little button, which will serve as a kind of hypnotic guide to "Buy Now."

Clearly this little "Buy Now/by now" game deploys an attempt to by-pass conscious thought and trigger reflexive buying by utilizing a phonetic trigger, which is supplemented by a visual cue which draws people's attention by a flickering light that is observed beneath a visitor's consciousness.

Clever, huh?

The nice young lady makes a few interesting comments under her video, like *when your efforts and intentions are to get someone to see that value in something that will benefit them, I think it's a totally COOL and ethical.... AND worthwhile subject to study if you like this type of information."* This is kind of like the "seller knows best" syndrome I mentioned before. They believe something is good for people, so they manipulate them to buy it.

She then writes something even more telling, *"More importantly to the person who thinks 'sales' is unethical or that I'm a part of a government run mind control operation. Relax. If you ever tried to get your spouse, children, or dog to see things your way and take action on something you were presenting, you are in 'sales.'"*

Mind control? Government? No. Mind Control? Sales? Yes. So why should we worry?

Does being hypnotized by a private individual representing a private company make you feel a lot less stressed than being hypnotized by a government eager to have compliant citizens? I mean isn't there a happy benefit to not having to make tough decisions over what you want to buy? How could anyone dare think this might be an attack on your personal liberties?

Sandra E. LaFlamme

As mentioned the blinking pixel trick is very much like the sub-liminal advertising techniques that allowed persuasive text to be flashed on a movie screen faster than the conscious mind could see but capable of being absorbed by the subconscious mind. This technique became famous back in 1957 when Vance Packard broadcast this "secret" to the public in his expose and best-selling book, *The Hidden Persuaders*.

This curious little manipulation of consumer's unconscious through some blinking pixels is a type of subliminal advertising, described as follows in an article on the subject described by Philip Merikle from the Department of Psychology in the University of Waterloo:

> A form of subliminal messaging commonly believed to exist involves the insertion of "hidden" messages into movies and TV programs. The concept of "moving pictures" relies on persistence of vision to create the illusion of movement in a series of images projected at 23 to 30 frames per second; the popular theory of subliminal messages usually suggests that subliminal commands can be inserted into this sequence at the rate of perhaps 1 frame in 25 (or roughly 1 frame per second). The hidden command in a single frame will flash across the screen so quickly that it is not consciously perceived, but the command will supposedly appeal to the subconscious mind of the viewer, and thus have some measurable effect in terms of behavior.[4]

Here are a few of the current books utilizing manipulative psychology, inspired by NLP or with a like-minded strategy, utilizing neuro-science or just plain psychology to trick the customer into buying:

When Do Consumers Become Money-Carrying Rats?

Author Drew Erick Whitman has the answer in his book, *Brain Scripts for Sales Success- 21 Hidden Principles of Consumer Psychology for Winning New Customers*. Whitman begins with this startling revelation:

> A highly skilled salesperson is not just somebody who knows the product and wants to sell you his or her stuff… That sales person is a scientist in a laboratory. To him or to her, you are a money-carrying rat.[5]

Now we know <u>anytime</u> we are in the presence of a highly skilled salesman, we become a sales laboratory rat.

But even with all that going for them, Whitman says that the normal, high-powered salesman cannot hold a candle to the psychologically-trained sales person who can:

> use the powerful techniques of consumer psychology to get inside their prospects' heads. They know how to persuade them to sign contracts, pull out credit cards and fork over crash.[6]

Whitman compares the ordinary but high-powered salesman to a man going to battle with a .38 special. Why use this low-level weapon when "a six-barreled 7.62-mm, 6000-round-per-minute mini-gun was available?" He suggests to his readers that only a fool would keep using the tiny pistols when they could "grab the bullet-showering beast."[7] Whitman's psychologically engineered brain scripts will therefore help you shower your customer's brains with these wondrous psychological bullets….

I realize that metaphors relating marketing and warfare are popular. After all isn't Sun Zu's "The Art of Warfare" been used for decades to win the hearts of clients by exercising guerilla strategies? And yes, of course there is "guerilla marketing" based on the idea of using military strategy to deal with an overwhelmingly large competitor. And in these somewhat combative thoughts, there is often a "Robin Hood" justification. And perhaps special strategies are needed for a Mom and Pop competing with a Walmart or Best Buy? But do we need combat metaphors in personal sales, especially using covert techniques most properly used in psychological warfare? Can nurturing, supportive efforts can produce worthwhile results, trumping Black Hat hypnotic and deceptive techniques? Is your faith in the God, the universe, and yourself big enough to envision this possibility?

Justifying Black Hat Tactics with Orwellian Mindtraps

Nowadays if we were to search for prophetic accuracy outside of an evangelical matrix, George Orwell would probably win hands down. In his dystopian masterpiece, *1984*, he describes the upside-down totalitarian language of Big Brother as Doublethink. He defines as "the power of holding two contradictory beliefs in one's mind simultaneously and accepting both of them."

For instance when you talk about practices being manipulative or exploitative, you generally think of deceptive practices, which lure people into making decisions on behalf of one person, not the other.

For instance confidence men are criminals whose trademark practice is to lure you into trusting them.

Now given what we have discussed so far, it is interesting that people who practice NLP often like to tout its virtues and the ethical virtues of its practices. In the introduction to the *NLP Sales Book- Your Guide to NLP Sales Techniques,* Ryan Camana, who describes himself as a master hypnotist, master NLP practitioner, trainer, and coach says very clearly that NLP is not manipulative or underhanded and that the word sales comes from the word serve and the top sales people in the world see themselves as servants, not exploiters. He says that "selling has nothing to do with manipulation" and then goes into a long explanation of the processes of mirror and matching, imitating people's bodily gestures, mirroring the sensory quality of their phrases, mimicking the tonality of the voice, in other words, subtly and quietly inducing a trance state, which makes them feel comfortable in their presence.[7]

Are you happy, even entranced, by the idea that since sales is supposedly coming from a word meaning "serve," no matter how we are manipulated, it's all OK? Still the writer seems to think all this is justified by the "servant" status of the seller. Do these assertions by the writer seem to suggest the Orwellian double speak of 1984? As a sales practitioner, how should we handle this type of salesperson when we show up in the role of consumer (which we all are, anyway)?

But as many practitioners of this ilk know, these techniques make clients very suggestible and more easily to lead into certain areas without due reflection. So if you're looking to put people into a trance state so they will be more easily led to make a purchase suggested by the sales practitioner, then it is a manipulation, not a rapport-building tool. I believe you will be failing very short in long-term success.

Gregory David, who wrote a book called *Selling: the Art and Science of Manipulation*, and coaches his readers in NLP and speaks exuberantly about the gentle art of mirroring, writes about integrity and tells us to "remember, sincerity sells."[8] Will your client really believe you better when while they're scratching their nose, you're reaching for your own? You can pick your nose, your client can pick their nose, but as the joke goes, you can't pick your client's nose.

Does Liberty Belong to the Few or the Many?

As this type of Black Hat system flourishes, and by all I can surmise, continues to grow, I believe it causes confusion by not addressing our own core issues with building meaningful relationships. Why is it tolerated or even courted as a legitimate method of sales? Growth with a solid core value set always leads to success in every area of your life. You don't leave behind your family on the way to business prosperity.

I would point out that we may have lost or never found a true appreciation for personal liberty. A lover of liberty, and this passion was very much alive in our Founding Fathers, although perhaps in a somewhat embryonic form, values liberty for all men and does not selfishly appropriate liberty for oneself. Social mores are not more important than high moral standing. Mores are important to understand, and Liberty gives you the freedom to be understanding while standing on solid ground. In the United States of America, I believe this is the ultimate trump card in our shared heritage.

• • • • •

> **Does Black Hat Marketing contribute to the destruction of American culture? Does it have implications for our political life? We have some wonderful information from neuroscience that can help protect our ability to make decisions. Do you think this type of Black Hat sales is a proper use of that information?**

• • • • •

Hypnotic induction deprives people of making thoughtful choices, which are at the very core of personal liberty, both the sales practitioner and the client's.

To wish, design, and implement methodologies to destroy the ability of a person to make reflective choices is not only an abuse of conscience, but it is downright unpatriotic. We do not want a bunch of brainwashed consumers running around our country in a manner perpetuated, endorsed, or activated by either the private or public sector. Besides since the same techniques that work on buying things and services you don't need, they also work on buying politicians that don't represent you but rather special interests who finance their campaigns. In this case, by brainwashing the voter, these special interests get the government to buy their products and services or fund their projects that, again, serve their own interest and not the public. Government waste is when governments buy things that they and the public really don't need.

We don't need private or public organizations utilizing this kind of consumer or citizen manipulation. Let's spread real wealth, not hypnotized fantasy wealth, <u>which takes ownership of policies</u>, products, or services that have no real value unless value means conflict, confusion, and loss.

The ability to effect commercial transactions, as I have mentioned, is an essential aspect of human nature and also a vital component of liberty and must be protected. Not for the chosen few but for everyone. And not for products or policies that don't work.

We need this White Hat sales paradigm, whatever you want to call it, as a watchword for all we do in American commerce and politics.

· · · · ·

Were you aware prior to reading this about NLP (Neuro-Linguistic Programming) hypnotic selling? Did you know or assume the reality of this degree of brainwashing we have presented in this chapter?

· · · · ·

END NOTES

1. Dr. Donald J. Moine, "Hypnotic Selling Techniques," Selling-Power.com
    http://www.sellingpower.com/content/article/?a=3909/hypnotic-selling-techniques

2. Ibid.

3. Ibid.

4. Philip Merickle, Department of Psychology, University of Waterloo, "Subliminal Advertising," *PsychologistWorld.com* *http://www.psychologistworld.com/influence_personality/subliminalads.php*

4. Drew Erick Whitman, *Brain Scripts for Sales Success- 21 Hidden Principles of Consumer Psychology for Winning New Customers* (Pennsylvania Plaza, New York: McGraw-Hill Education, 2014), p. 1

5. Ibid., p. 2

6. Ibid, p. 3

7. Ryan Camana, *NLP Sales Book- Your Guide to NLP Sales Techniques* (Amazon Digital Services: Camana Enterprises LLC, 2014)

8. Gregory David, *Selling: the Art and Science of Manipulation* (Amazon Digital Services, 2015)

Chapter 6

YOUR WHITE HAT IMAGE
Science, Technology, and Authenticity

Having been involved in many sales systems and the process of sales for many years, I am highly familiar with recent changes, which are now impacting heavily on the nature of contemporary sales. To me there are two main components.

The first component is, of course, the Internet, to which with such robust entities as Skype, Facebook, Google Hangouts, and other such audio and video programs. In fact many things can be sold face-to-face- virtually, through the Internet, in a manner quite new in the history of sales. Less work than going door-to-door. I'm not always sure that's such a good thing. A person with a toe- to-toe experience is never at the mercy of a person with a theory. A virtual face-to-face understanding does not capture authentic human familiarity. There is experience in selling, say, on Skype. It is virtual, face-to-face, but does not encompass breathing the same air as the person with whom you are working. If you are near a pig farm and you note, "It smells like money around here," then your comment will be in line with what the farm neighbors household understands. The value of this personal exercise cannot be overlooked. Knowing neighborhoods, floor plans, and views is the living component that still needs to be provided in real estate sales. Real products need to be given relative value by real experience. The internet provides dynamic avenues to form meaningful conversations which lead to transactions of homes to custom shirts.

Beyond those strictly computer Internet possibilities, with the evolution and migration of the Internet to mobile phones and other devices, sales practitioners should continually look for opportunities of direct contact.

Another aspect of the Internet is, of course, the advertising and prospecting functions that have a possible immediacy and affordability that is also an enjoyable new addition to sales efforts given the many cumbersome efforts involved in the former sales process (I guess there are some advantages of not going door-to-door).

The second component of the major shift in sales systems is progressing with the new contributions of neuroscience, a science which includes many interesting bedfellows called by various names. Cognitive neuroscience deals with how the brain creates and controls our thoughts and language, assists with problem-solving and utilizes its memory functions, cognitive linguistics, an offshoot of this cognitive neuroscience tracks language and its relationship to brain functions, casting unexpected light on how we are influenced by our peers, environment, and media. Frame and narrative theory have evolved from this understanding, which as we point out in this book is critical to understanding how we make decisions.

Neuroscience has given us the possibility of understanding the psychology of sales much better but also the capacity to manipulate the process more easily, often with selfish motives. My system of selling, *White Hat Sales*, will not only benefit and profit those who use it but also serve as an antidote to the bitter experience some have had with sales training that focuses on tricky, deceptive sales techniques for the purpose of self-aggrandizement by the salesperson and their company at the expense of the client.

The techniques deploying neuroscience that I am focusing on, both good and bad, are not subliminal or hypnotic techniques but rather ones that capitalize on somewhat new experiments that show a proclivity for people to favor certain types of narratives, including sales narratives not as a result of reasoning but rather as a result of unexamined biases built into our neurophysiology apparently made to protect us instinctively but also a tremendous barrier to reasoned consideration of a purchase or a negotiation.

Sales Techniques and Science
Don't Hang Your Hat on It!

It is true that our platform does utilize some understanding of neuroscience, but we are not going to totally hang our hat on it. Maybe a little bit. We are prepared to stick it there for a while, but our eagle eye is on that hat rack.

Here's why…

Although we mention and are influenced by certain experiments and points of view represented by the rapidly developing cognitive sciences, we need to emphasize that the techniques and applications we stress do not simply rely on scientific studies, which often rapidly change over a period of time. For instance in the early days of astronomy, there was this progression: first there was the Ptolemaic system (based on Ptolemy, the Greek astronomer and mathematician). Ptolemy thought the Sun went around the Earth in a circle but not in a straight line (or pure circumference). Instead Ptolemy thought the Sun travelled around the sun in a circle, interrupted by a number of "epicycle" or tiny extra circles it made in its path.

Sandra E. LaFlamme

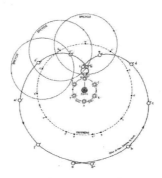

Epicycles in Ptolemy

When the great Copernicus created his controversial theory of the Earth going around the Sun (for which Galileo, a supporter of the Copernican theory, did some jail time), he also used the idea of epicycles, only this time it was the Earth doing the epicycles. Copernicus's breakthrough was that his model had LESS EPICYCLES THAN PTOLEMY. So Copernicus was wrong! Very wrong! Neither the Sun nor the Earth move in epicycles ever!

So in those days, with their limited telescopes and astronomy, the improvement of the mathematical models actually favored an epicycle model, even though it was dead wrong.

But if nothing else, at least Copernicus got it right about the Earth travelling around the Sun. And this made the Vatican very upset, and as a supporter of Copernicus, Galileo soon found himself in prison, feeling compelled to recant from his heresy (probably when he got really tired of prison food).

But regardless of the Vatican's opinion, mankind was ultimately stripped of its throne in the center of the universe because in not too much time, the model was about to shift again!

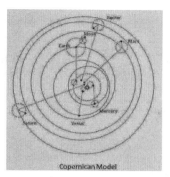

Epicycles in Copernicus

Yep, along came along Kepler, whose work firmly rested on these early discoveries. And he made everything more elegant by postulating that the Earth went around the Sun in an elliptical (or oval, egg-shaped) path. And now even the Sun was not really in the center of it all but kind of off to one side in the middle of the ellipse.

In other words, nature, certain through divine machinations (as Kepler would say), had a much more real world elegant way of moving things than Ptolemy or Copernicus. I know this was a big breakthrough, but all Kepler did was discover something that already existed.

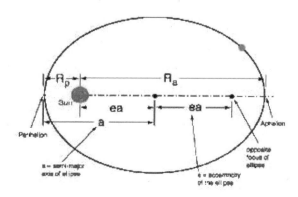

Kepler Elliptical Model

But during the time that these three scientists were functioning, they were, in my belief, sincerely trying to explain nature as they understood it. To the extent Ptolemy and Copernicus were wrong, it was because their perspective and science were limited.

I bring this up because neuroscience is a relatively young discipline, and what we think we have today may be displaced and reinterpreted in the future. But yes, we have a lot of people in various sales and marketing systems, not typically invested in hard science, jumping on the bandwagon.

But things may change, and I predict in the near future, debate may change the paradigms we are trusting in the present, and yes, debate is probably going on right now about many areas. This is what science is all about.

It is a tool for finding truth in nature, but it is a tool that is continuously changing, often in a good sense but sometimes takes wrong turns. Just look at the history of atomic theory. Compare Dalton's atomic theory of matter with Quantum Physics. Compare Newtonian Physics with Einstein's Theory of Relativity.

In fact the FLAME Training Sales System and White Hat Sales System is based on a lot more than ephemeral science, although properly used, the current knowledge we have is eye-opening and incredibly useful, even revelational, about how the human mind works. Still science is not the really solid foundation of the system.

Whether or not reflexive and reflective narratives can be compared neurologically does not change the reality that people often are acting on unspoken and often wrong assumptions spontaneously and do not give themselves time to reflect. And sometimes when they reflect carefully, they are sometimes reflecting with wrong assumptions.

For instance I often have problems with clients about their pricing of a home, not because they aren't thinking about the price they want reflectively but because they are using the pricing they are familiar with in a different market or from past pricing that they experienced in the past.

These clients, if they are serious and rational, are often happy to learn from me the realities of the market and are able to relate to a price on the buying and selling of a home in a perfectly calm and appropriate way, whether the price is too much or too little.

FLAME and White Hat Sales are securely based on the idea that mankind is endowed with a conscience, a quality of conscience linked to the Creator and fully good in its pure, uncorrupted nature. Jefferson said, "We are endowed by our Creator with certain inalienable rights, and among those are life, liberty, and the pursuit of happiness." We agree, but we would go further.

Besides being endowed with inalienable rights, whose importance is inestimable, we are also endowed with a profound spiritual capacity, a spiritual power also of inestimable importance and one, unlike science, that does not intrinsically change.

This capacity is nothing less than the POWER TO DO GOOD, a power that reflects the sense in which mankind is made in the image of God. The ephemeral and ever-changing vicissitudes of science will not change that nor our faith in a Creator who has endowed us with certain rights as children of God.

White Hat Marketing is firmly based on these ideals, which are eternal and not subject just to the advances of science and its perennial ability to be either used to further the betterment of man or misused to foster mankind's ability to activate scenarios for the sake of greed, power, and notoriety.

● ● ● ● ●

Do you believe in the ability to do good trumping any kind proposed methodology to ability to manipulate people for profit? Sometimes we find that people have ethics in their personal life, but they leave them at home when they are doing business. What do you really think? Can doing good surpass doing evil in the marketplace?

• • • • •

My recent success in blogging mainly about real estate sales and activities is based on actually looking around and finally being able to communicate what I have found in the real world of what is going on in my sales transactions. The fact that I have learned to communicate the basis of that level of mastery is proven by the happy reviews I have received from my clients, chronicling their success with the sales processes they have absorbed for personal benefit.

So now let's turn the focus on you, the role you are playing as you carry out the sales process, the commissions you are earning but also the ones you have not been earning because you have not yet learned to apply the processes discussed in this book, the processes that lead to REAL SALES and REAL SUCCESS in this difficult, challenging, but often amazingly rewarding REAL WORLD!

Be Nice but Be Real
HOW AUTHENTICITY PAYS OFF

Networking is part of sales. You can network without sales, but you can't sell without networking. Guaranteed!

If everyone needs to network, then everyone needs to hear and say NO elegantly. Because although you may be networking primarily to sell, so also may the contacts you find on your journey.

Networking is an art, and maybe the essence of that art is the art of asking questions. People love to be asked questions, for it means that someone out there in that confusing world wants actually to know something about them.

If you have networking on the mind, then good! How you are wiring your brain network for the networking event is where your authenticity comes from.

For that reason, asking questions is the first thing you do after introducing yourselves to a fresh contact. And just like you do with the introduction, the questions, and everything else, you try and keep your demeanor bright and friendly, not phony but certainly positive and light. After all you are on a treasure hunt, filled with the possibility that you will truly run into a beautiful string of pearls or perhaps some nice big blocks of gold bullion, metaphors of course, for that really big connection and that really big sale.

The saying, "It may seem as if I'm being nice, but I'm actually just networking" is funny and true.

• • • • •

Why is authenticity so important in sales?

How can "being nice" hurt you in the long run?

How do you feel when you feel someone is faking their real feelings or really doesn't care when they're selling you something? Is it really that hard to spot?

• • • • •

Year in and year out, sometimes forever, many people choose to communicate with others in the exact same way regardless of whether the times are good or bad. Like Little Johnny One Note, they put all their eggs in the Basket of Being Nice. The reality is that to other people, eventually it will be more like just *appearing* to be nice can lead to even established connections questioning your integrity and the reality of the relationship they have with you. When you are insincere, your voice and body language can give you away, sometimes not at first but eventually.

Sadly this will not take you very far for very long. Seeming to be nice and really being nice are two different things. In sales your lack of perceived authenticity will impact your paycheck big time. Not willing to be yourself can be a big risk.

I've always been in sales. Even when my full-time occupation was in computer consulting, I sold Amway Queen Cookware.

Zig Ziglar is my hero. He sold pots and pans door to door. How authentic can you get?

Face-to-face, Toe-to-toe with folks. You either know your stuff, demonstrate ability, and have a good call to action, or you starve! I have wanted to be like him since I was a teenager. My favorite saying of his is *"Timid Salespeople Have Skinny Kids."*

I'm not timid because of Zig, as well as my family's encouragement. When I was younger, I didn't value the differences between real nice and fake nice. I do now. I pay very close attention. I can work with anybody. And if I see a lack of communication springing up, I look to my demeanor.

Am I trying to be nice when I should be frank? Am I being overly friendly when I should at least be acknowledging I am being insulted? Posturing, instead of being real, could be costly to the deal. And being nice at the right time can be tempting because it supposedly diminishes the risk of conflict. If I see I am taking the easy way out, I then take extra steps to overcome any shortfall, generally based on my client's loss of confidence in my integrity. People can spot when you're faking, even if they don't realize it consciously.

• • • • •

> Why, although authenticity is so valuable, do many people think it is so risky? Do their assumptions of "risk" tell you anything about what they think are the nature of things?

• • • • •

I look at any loss of confidence that my client has developed during the sales process. This is my responsibility, my burden to overcome. Therefore I need to able to execute self-judgment without getting into toxic self-condemnation, which will only sabotage my mood and my efforts.

My attitude regarding compassionate self-judgment reflects my confidence in a loving God who created me in his image. As a creative force created by a powerful and caring God, I can tap into how I have been designed and use my voice to create confidence in the projects points we are facing in our transaction. My voice is naturally going to reflect my belief in success as I understand it. I choose to garner my energy to communicate forward solution-oriented actions.

But more specifically in terms of authenticity, the science we are discovering that has already been enlightened to us through our loving God. God helps me look at myself in a loving way.

Who we are as sales ppractitioners is an extension of who we believe ourselves to be. Our relationship with each other is exemplified by our relationship with our loving God.

Giving to others of yourself is easy if you freely receive from God. You aren't worried you will run out of supply, currency, and most especially love.

When we behave as if we have a shortage in these areas, it is because of fear. Real fearlessness allows you to know you are walking into a room filled with answers, insights, and understanding, even if two minutes before it had not fully manifested in your conscious mind.

• • • • •

Given our discussion of neuroscience, particularly in the area of frames and narratives, as contributing to the science of sales, do you think this can help you perfect your own sales processes?

• • • • •

So we find ourselves digging deeper into the unconscious and conscious mind to scientifically peel back layers of understanding to our wiring. Our brain is wired to our behavior. Neuroscience and psychology can gracefully collaborate together for a greater understanding of ourselves.

Now I pay closer attention to my patterns. Do you do what you say you're going to do? I do. I'm looking to be an attractive force for people who also demonstrate success patterns in their life. It's created a new level of profitability in every portion of my life.

Let me give you an example of the first time I realized there was a big gap in my understanding. If you can believe it, living next store to me in the first home I ever owned was a real life, dyed-in-the-wool drug dealer, Larry the Drug Guy.

I was a single woman at the time, with a predilection for fixing things and doing my own yard work. I made everything I possibly could. I jumped at the chance when I was offered to take part in a community project. I saw everyone who was my neighbor as an extension of my new wonderful experience. After all I owned a house in a real neighborhood and I wanted to play a part!

On Memorial Day weekend, I rented a 1.5" wood chipper. Mom and I planned to have a ton of fun throwing tree branches through this thing to make mulch for my garden. The preceding four weekends had been spent preparing. Hedging. Edging. Clipping. Trimming.

The garden supply store was set to deliver the chipper, but they were concerned for my safety. How could a single woman handle this level of danger?

They made me sign a waiver. They even made me buy a hard hat with a face shield. Now I also wanted to rent a chain saw, but this was too much for them, but they refused. I love those guys to this day, saving both my arms from the Monte Python Black Knight Syndrome.

So back at my home, I of course asked my neighbors if I could borrow their chainsaw. Really, I was that ridiculous. And then magic! My neighborhood drug dealer steps up. When he heard about my pitiful lack of chainsaw access, he offered to cut down as many extra tree limbs I could not accomplish with ordinary garden tools.

When he asked me, for a moment I thought I heard a certain tension in his voice, a granite hard coldness, and even a cruelty, but when I looked at his smiling, pleasant face, I kind of buried that impression. He wasn't Braer Fox, and I wasn't Braer Rabbit. This wasn't a briar path. It was my own yard, and I needed those limbs cut and here was this wonderful person proffering assistance.

In fact he seemed to be the nicest guy on the block. He was the only one offering to help. I wondered secretly if he was some kind of a saint. His kid played with the neighbor's grandchildren. That gave me a lot of points towards true neighbor authenticity.

Of course at the time, I didn't know my neighbor was a drug dealer. How could I not have known? I think I was just enchanted out of my mind at the wonder of his kind offer.

But when I look back, I really wonder at my judgment. There was more than one tell-tale sign.

His house was run down. He spent all afternoon on his front porch. He had a purple grow light gleaming from his basement. He had cars that came into his driveway from 11 P.M. to 4 A.M. for only minutes at a time. He has power tools. Lots and lots of lawn and power tools. Even though his yard looked like the 1979 Burlington, Iowa/Mississippi shoreline, nothing but mud with a blowup kiddie pool poking it's head up from the silt, I immaturely wanted to believe he was nice because he cut some branches for me. But observing all these patterns, I still didn't register the incongruity. I admit I never could locate his halo.

Speaking about what subject started this conversation, guess what determines whether a drug dealer can pay his mortgage? You got it! The size of his network. He's a trained networker. Like any real professional, he wants respect, he wants to move up in the ranks, and he is highly committed to his trade. He's viscerally friendly. Giving me what I asked for in power tool help. I'm the oblivious hard-working yard worker. What do I know?

In retrospect I wondered if I should have dismissed my initial instincts about him when he offered so freely to cut my branches. I had this slight suspicion that there was something chilly in his manner, despite his smile. Like maybe he was doing it as a down payment for some kind of future benefit. Like it was a kind of small investment in my confidence in him. Still I never let it bother me. The halo and everything.

But one spring day in his front yard, I think I got a peek at the man that he was.

At the time, I was mowing my front yard, and his front yard like one big horizontal line, back and forth about nine to twelve times. Each line was about 250 feet long. Why not?

The truth had come out, and neighbor had gone to jail for six to nine months, but I wasn't about to let my curb appeal go, too! My drug-dealing neighbor had gotten busted of course for saying no to the law.

So in the spirit of "I am my brother's keeper" and unconditional love and forgiveness, I mowed his front lawn. I was engaging in something helpful and fun for me. I was sowing good human effort as seed.

While making one of my half football field length mower passes, Larry the Drug Guy walked up to me and tapped me lightly on the shoulder. Being so transfixed on the grass height, speed, and accuracy of my work, I had not noticed him approaching. Accordingly I jumped over the moon inside but remained calm as I turned to see his sincerely kind face. For the first time, no hardness. No cunning. No "seeming" to be nice. Real. I didn't realize it at first, but he was about to make a confession.

Larry let it out, and what he said was bittersweet. I could see that he was upset and truly sorry. He explained that his role in the drug niche was basically pot and a few peripheral products, but he wasn't beholden to any evil drug lords, and what he did never led to violence nor did he believe it led to addiction, most of the time. But there were a few accidents here and there, but even they were somewhat minor. Still, during his "career," they had troubled him.

The real problem wasn't violence from his clients or his sources. It was the risks he took and the jail time, which ultimately led to the breakup of his family. After all that was laid out before me and he saw that I was sympathetic because of his contriteness, the subject changed, and for a while we began to share our personal lives, goals, and dreams. It really matters to me what happens to the humans around me. He could see that I cared and he relaxed.

Soon there was lots of laughter and camaraderie, especially when I began to point out his transferrable skills from skullduggery to a real job. After all wasn't he truly a powerful networker, considering the core of everything he had been doing was illegal and even broaching the nature of his inventory could be dangerous?

I told him about Amway and a dozen other side projects I had done. He told me about the clever way he sidled up to a customer, revealing himself very slowly and carefully, using maximum empathic melding to protect himself from revealing himself to the wrong person but also through discovering the best way to close the deal, if a deal was to be made. His sales technique was truly a synthesis between Zig Ziglar, my favorite sales mentor, and Mr. Spock.

"Wow!" I said, "Your sales technique is awesome, and I have never heard anything like your mind meld technique in the literature."

He blushed for a moment or two.

"If you were selling medical equipment instead of handfuls of pot, I bet you would have an amazing 401K by now (this was before everyone lost their shirt in the global financial meltdown to come)."

When he heard this, his eyes shot wide open.

"Really?" he asked.

"Yep, you are a natural born salesman, Larry. Properly focused, your ability could bring you a leg up in the legal free enterprise market place."

I could see from his expression that this was all new to him. I particularly noted his fascination with the word legal. Could you really make that kind of money *legally?* It was a fascinating idea for someone who mostly played video games since he was six and never read the financial columns.

The outstanding part for my personal growth and understanding was realizing how Larry viewed his occupation. He viewed it like any other occupation. We are talking here about basic laws of the universe, at least those that apply to business.

Yes, criminals use networking to rob banks, launder money, and settle debts violently. Toxic dictators use networking in their unscrupulous business deals with other countries. Avaricious CEOs use networking to fill up their illegitimate bonuses stolen from the shareholders. So why shouldn't Larry do it?

Better still why don't we all do it legally? Because when you do, *thar is gold in them thar hills!*

How about you? What are your motivations? How do you customize your interests, motivations, and over-all purpose in business to a networking protocol?

Remember one of the supreme efforts made nowadays is the networking that takes place in social media. This may be one step removed from a face-to-face networking club, but if done correctly, it can be very powerful.

In certain businesses, live networking is still important. It is not inappropriate for certain salespeople or account executives to travel to their key accounts or key prospects by car or even by airplane. But nowadays everyone uses social networking to some degree.

Networking should be part of your life, something you should do every week. When you do, don't make the networking confrontation about yourself. Make it about building a deeper relationship with your new contact, asking many questions, trying to learn as much about the contact as possible, remembering that people are typically extremely interested in themselves, and that is not necessarily wrong because caring about your own life counts for something big. Otherwise why are we told to "Love thy neighbor as thyself?"

"Thyself" counts for you, but it also counts for the people you are networking with.

Since often networking works with lightening-like speed, your opportunity to make a great impression may be limited to a few minutes. And depending what you are presenting and in what venue you are presenting it, you may actually be asking for a sale or at least to find out that there might be an interest in a sale. That means that a "yes" or a "no" may be eminent.

Most of us can handle a yes fairly evenly, as long as we don't start jumping up and down and screaming "hallelujah" or some such thing that belongs in either a church or a teenage cheerleading rally. Yes should prompt you instead to pay attention to the details of the sale and the service to the customer. Be grateful, polite, and finish up quickly all the paperwork, but keep your dignity. By the way, hearing the first yes in this way during a presentation is a mark of a top-notch professional.

On the other hand, many networkers and sales people do not know how to handle NOs, and that is what this book is all about. Ask yourself right now, after you introduce yourself, how do you handle a silent or awkward NO? Are you nice or genuinely nice, bringing elegance to your counterpart? Without seeming like a robot, how do our mentally gear up for this? How do you handle a no without seeming formulaic or distant or angry?

Realize above all NO does not necessarily mean forever. And unless the contact involved has contradicted themselves by changing their mind inappropriately or has been unnecessarily rude or has showed bad intentions, you may want to keep him as a prospect. Sometimes a sale can take weeks or even years.

Besides getting into more definitive ways of acting and thinking about nos, you need to examine your general emotional and physical condition. What company are you keeping? Are you busted and disgusted, or are you having fun? What are ways you can have fun and be engaging?

Hearing and saying no elegantly will help with the proper focus, attention, and ability to do so legitimately and profitably. But this will only be relatively easy and comfortable if you are that way in general within yourself. A healthy, positive, and nurturing lifestyle will keep you on track in sales.

So this is something to think about, too.

Protecting Your Image

If you have a big problem, the first step is certainly not to broadcast it to colleagues, friends, and even worse, clients. The smartest thing to do is to give yourself some space and begin to work through your problem, yourself even if you know you have resources if you need more help. To solve real problems, it is best to be centered and careful about your solution. Do your best to analyze it and then test out various solutions until you find the one that makes the most sense, even if it includes reaching out. Broadcasting problems with your mouth instead of using your eyes and ears can lead to premature, panic-oriented solutions since you may be settling on ill-considered solutions other than your own. You should own the solution you settle with lock, stock, and barrel.

In White Hat Sales, you need to be the problem-solver, not the anxiety-ridden, insecure bearer of your own bad news. This means more than just "positive thinking." It means real self-confidence.

Outside of reality TV, there is no reward for the big long list of problems. And by the way, in reality TV, the biggest reward is for the producers who find narcissistic kids who rant about their problems. That's entertainment? Not for me, but by the prolific opportunities for reality and talk show options, there is big reward in packaging these emotions. You are not here to create sympathy in order to make the sale. You are using empathy to determine how to make the sale if the sale is right.

• • • • •

> **What is the best image to present to clients? How do you do this with integrity and authenticity?**

• • • • •

One of the mistakes people sometimes make who are negotiating salaries is that they will discuss their critical need for the job, how they want to make more money, and how they need special accommodations for their schedule. Although sometimes this may be appropriate, at least in part, the role of the job seeker that should be projected to the prospective employer is that of a time-saver, moneymaker, and a problem-solver. His problems, not yours.

Crying at the drop of the hat is appropriate for an actress. Not anyone else. Certainly not clients or prospective employers.

So in White Hat Sales, we are focused on the client's needs, not our own. That is a form of selflessness and it should be cultivated whenever possible.

• • • • •

> **How do you protect your image and avoid being a panic-driven, anxiety-prone practitioner? Do you think it is ever appropriate to beg, and if you did, what are the consequences?**

Chapter 7

THE MOST POWERFUL WAY TO BUILD CLIENT RAPPORT

As Socrates said, "The unexamined life is not worth living."

As far as I am concerned, Socrates is right, and continuous self-evaluation is the key to the successful life of a sales person. So going back to that second magic word, how does the anticipation of NO make you feel in each and every circumstance you can think of? Can you see that how you think about it can influence every decision, word, action, and physical reaction you make? In *Who Switched Off My Brain?*[1] Neuroscientist Dr. Caroline Leaf explains that these thoughts are measurable and occupy mental *"real estate."*

· · · · ·

Why should sales practitioners constantly evaluate their sales encounters and presentations? Prior to reading this book, what was your protocol for self-evaluation?

· · · · ·

Depression and anger cause stress. So do other emotions, like fear or jealousy or a desire for physical revenge (not a good thing). Every system in your body is involved when you let stress run rampant. It can be triggered if you don't know yourself very well. It can be triggered if you don't know your product. Or it can be triggered if you don't know the market.

· · · · ·

Do you have small or large battles within yourself with these types of emotions? Can you give some examples of how these emotions have affected your inner life and your performance at work? Why do you need to overcome anger and depression in order to really operate on your highest level of performance?

· · · · ·

Now we have discussed preparing for a sales situation such as I do regularly with an open house, we can also ask ourselves a bigger question after the work is over with, "How well did I really prepare for the day?"

Human beings are always interacting, always networking with friends, family, with clerks at the grocery store, with lawyers, teachers, gymnastic coaches, etc. *So how did you do today?* is something you might ask yourself at the end of the day.

· · · · ·

> **Can you live with this kind of self-discipline? Do you regard as possibly a powerful tool for working forward in your own sales? Why does White Hat Sales stress self-evaluation as a major part of the sales process?**

Now getting back to the sales discussion.

Taking the time to get up to speed on all your preparation will allow you to step outside yourself and hear what is genuinely being said. No matter how much candy coating is going on, if you know your product, the market, yourself, and the opportunity, you will be able to hear what you need to and find a way to help. Helping is building your pipeline. Know what direction you are helping others towards and actually communicate to them what they need to know. That's sales school 101.

Here is an exercise. What would say about this room? Can you add perspective with your personal insight?

What colors would you add? Is this big enough for one of your large holiday parties? Can you imagine the flow from inside to outside and all around the kitchen and pool? What about beyond, is there a volleyball court, tennis court or beach front?

Does a picture say 1,000 words?

Or did you just have one word? If so was it oozing with emotion? Or did the judgment of the color orange stop you?

Think of your client's reaction? Can you pick up on what his words really mean? What does his body language say about what he just seen? What does it say about the meaning of his words? If you aren't aware of current trends in this area from which your client comes, you may put your judgment in front of receiving insights from your client.

The World is Your Stage!

When you are selling, you are always on stage, but although certain components of what you say may be memorized to assure factual consistency, most of what you say is going to improvisational and contextual, depending on the responsiveness of the client to your presentation, be it formal or informal (there are gradations). Therefore it doesn't matter what your opinion is when "on stage" but knowing the situation so well that you make no mistakes in understanding the circumstances.

So after you are through with cursory introductions, you need to be very aware of yourself. As Shakespeare says, "All the world's a stage." Well, you are now on it. And you need to stay in character.

· · · · ·

What aspect of presentations should you memorize?

Why is it important to be improvisational in sales, and what do you need to do to be able to do that?

· · · · ·

Yes, as a practitioner, you are on stage. And in this sense, you are an actor, and in this play, you are the protagonist, the lead character.

But in all dramatic productions, the play's story and character are really shaped by the playwright. And in this story, just like Shakespeare, you are not only a playwright and an actor but also (unlike the renowned bard), you get to both play and shape in the main character.

This shouldn't be so much trouble. Because in this case, the true character is your authentic self.

So you make your presentation and particularly when you make a pitch (actually promote action on the part of the client to make a commitment) and get any kind of response but particularly a Big Bad NO, you should some time later, perhaps after work, initiate a self-evaluation. This is similar to a great actor or a great musician evaluating his performance. You never stop learning and you must never stop evaluating. Maybe you and your team are at the top of your game, and your audience just doesn't know enough about you.

Just like any other actor.

What?! Are you going to leave this evaluation to the critics? No! No! No! Serious actors may listen to the critics, but they know that the real game changer is what they themselves thought about their performance, weighing audience, critical response but mostly their own experience and self-knowledge.

Did you appear nervous? Non-attentive? Lackluster in your interest? Underwhelming? Did you experience a strong fear, or in some cases, unnecessary or premature exhilaration before the close, which gave the final NO a bigger bite.

This is where self-study must come in to win the day. And self-study is not the same as it was thirty years ago. Neuroscience is filling the gap in our understanding of the brain but also adding to the complexity of the marketing paradigms because neuroscience can be significantly abused.

> Who is your most important critic? A) Your sales manager?
> B) Friends and Family C) Your client D) You In evaluating
> yourself, what deficiencies are you most concerned about,
> and how do you think you can spot them? Why should you
> particularly focus on what happens to both the client and
> yourself when they say no?

• • • • •

We have been pointing out throughout this book that neuroscience, although adding immeasurably to our scientific understanding of our own minds, can be abused in a way more sophisticated than the simplistic closing tactics and soft-spoken confidence-producing

And so much of it, through the largesse of modern political and commercial marketing, as well in some of the newer, extremely helpful, psychological therapies and sales systems (like ours) is working to drive our behavior way underground, hidden below consciousness, where science has told us most of the action is.

For those of you who are familiar with anger management techniques, some of those stratagems are predicated on detecting the underlining thoughts or narratives that gives one a justification for anger. As neuroscientists tell us these days, 95% of our "thinking" and "emotions" are unconscious. Anger reactions may be attuned to thought, but they come fast and furious, and most often the anger has been accepted as a normal response until it becomes so fraught with consequences that the habitual offender runs to an anger management course to save him or herself, unless of course he ordered to go as appointed by a court.

Actually any thought or emotion can become addictive, and in the case of anger or depression triggered by rejection, the real thinking behind the emotions is hidden. Worse these types of emotions lead to further rejection and deepening reactions. The fact is if you focus on NO as a negative, it becomes toxic. It can then poison that specific sale or it can poison all future sales. How much damage it can do is contextual. It depends on the situation.

If your position with a product or service requires you to grow and change, then you want to watch how NO makes you feel. If the price is too high and you can't control it, you may feel betrayed by the company or person who is controlling the sale. If the product is changed so as, by your standards and judgment, to dramatically lower its usefulness or value, you may be extremely distrustful of doing business with that person or company anymore or feel trapped because you can't move away very comfortably and have to live with the situation. How do you adjust to what may very well be actual, real betrayal, stupidity, or even maliciousness by persons involved in a sale?

Not with toxic anger and not with depression to be sure. For real success, you will want your reaction to be driven by a combination of self-esteem, empathy, and caution as you develop the best strategy possible.

And sometimes the best strategy is to say nothing and concentrate on future goals, perhaps with circumstances and conditions more under your control.

Silence, then in this context, is for you to move on.

We have been discussing how to act when those who control the terms of your selling, like the company or supervisors above you, do things that might constitute absolute deception and betrayal.

And it is true, sometimes because of the circumstance means remaining silent, and more or less, choosing your weapons and deciding if you should use them. By weapons I mean formal complaints to the higher echelons in a company or even a government agency, a serious personal confrontation perhaps with other people present (as in a sales meeting) or even terminating your employment in a way with consequences for your employer (like not finishing certain specific tasks relevant to your position because you will not tolerate to be treated this way).

Of course there are times that may not be nearly extreme and then quick, perhaps almost improvised, communication is important. This can be face-to face, but if you are not physically present but on the phone, you will want to. If you are not physically present but on the phone, you will want to respond with a sound or word that represents a sentiment of relationships. Communication with connectedness is not concession. So it is very important that you enlist your hearing and saying elegant focused summary words.

There is a difference between shooting a person because you hate them or want to see them suffer and shooting a person because they are about to shoot you or kill someone you love. Your words will have the same effect. Believe it or not, you can act righteously with physical violence without all the extra toxic emotional trappings of hatred and revenge.

Moving away from a client that represents ill will is taking action by moving on with silence. If you have decided that the level in which the client is engaging offers no possible outcome but destruction to your business, do not mirror their emotion. To do so would be like shooting them and yourself at the same time, thereby multiplying the affect of the negative emotion.

In the days long good-bye, children were treated to this a kind of non-retributive righteousness by cowboy heroes, such as Gene Autry, Roy Rogers, and Hopalong Cassidy to name a few. These cowboys were concerned with justice not revenge and retribution in dealing with bad guys.

I believe there is a kind of righteous anger, which prompts one to act against injustice, which does not really contain the seeds of hatred and retribution that other forms of anger do, perhaps embodied in the characters of the original Lone Ranger and Tonto. But speaking of the recent Johnny Depp film (he played Tonto), *does the Lone Ranger really ride again?*

More recent generations were treated to less righteous prototypes, like Clint Eastwood as *Dirty Harry* or Charles Bronson as Paul Kersey in the *Death Wish* film series. And more recently, TV "heroes" like Kiefer Sutherland who played Jack Bauer in *24* or Ben McKenzie who plays James Gordon in the series featuring the young Bruce Wayne, *Gotham*. Indeed the Batman films featuring Batman glorify hatred and revenge, emotions somewhat found in the original comic book but now seriously enhanced. Nowadays the exaltation of revenge, toxic anger, and even politically sanctioned torture has blurred any kind of moral distinction between types of anger.

Keeping Emotions Out

Empathy is great, but it doesn't mean that, as an agent with clients, you do not have to sometimes handle with kid gloves the emotions of your clients and the consequences of their expression.

In fact I watched a deal blow up last week because the prospective buyer did not use the word NO in a respectful way. The sellers resented it, and it ultimately caused enough ill will to derail the deal.

The biggest career-enhancing maneuver I make is keeping the emotional tone of my client's words in the room and away from the ears of others.

· · · · ·

> Emotions can be positive or negative, but sometimes you want to get them entirely out of the picture. Can you give examples from your own experience? How and why?

· · · · ·

Here is an example from my world: the seller may need to ask for occupancy after closing or hold onto the product after they have received money. This potentially means a rental time or a couple days of grace. Whatever it is, respect is necessary for everyone. All the parties are making big moves, spending their time, money, and energy to maneuver their life in the way they think best.

But if You Can Deploy it, Empathy is Best

The way out of a lot of problems with clients is to use empathy, perhaps the most powerful and most underused tool in those involved in buying and selling. So with that state of mind and heart, let's put your client's shoes on for a moment. Do they see you as their trusted advisor? If yes they will want to show their trust in you by exposing their emotions and true concerns to you.

· · · · ·

> Are you a naturally empathic person, or are you someone who does have trouble stepping into another person's moccasins? In what way would you like to further your ability to be empathic?

· · · · ·

Yes, of course your clients are afraid of getting a NO, but they must see that you are not. That's what helps build trust. You work through these situations everyday, and you know!

As you begin to get comfortable in their shoes, you see that they are afraid of the chaos created by not asking for a little extra time. Let them be emotional You be calm. No matter what the known facts are, your value goes up the more you keep your tone respectful. Keeping your thinking logical and linear will add profitability to the relationship, and trust.

Often times sales are blocked because either you or your clients do not bring up important concerns. This is over because if you do, such as you pointing out a defect in the timing of a sale or in the product or itself or the client not mentioning that your solution is objectionable for personal and subjective reasons that they don't want to mention.

The real demon behind many of these interactions is FEAR. Fear is the enemy of logic and reason. It bubbles up in the psyche because of human's instinctive nature, a survival mechanism that needs concentration and reflection, primary mechanisms of self-examination as a countermeasure in order to rule the psyche consciously.

Being the logical force in a tornado of fear sprinkled with technical and legal verbal gymnastics is of immense benefit in real estate and other buyer/seller transactions where the buyer's ability to confidently make decisions is challenged. Lawyers strive for this role every day. So do realtors, accountants, and talent agents for that matter. But handling things with logic, ethics, and self confidence will always be your goal with clients. Often in the world of clients and their counterparts, you may be the only one who keeps it calm and puts it all together. You will be the one whose business profits, and everyone else with feel the warmth of your collaborative embrace. If you can make it to this level, everyone wins, and your business grows quickly from referrals.

• • • • •

Be as honest as you can. What role does fear play in your inner life? As a sales practitioner, do you use fear to sway your clients to buy?

• • • • •

When trouble beckons and the answer really is NO, then don't jump the gun and **bust** them with the bad news. Explore, probe, and delve into the top most feasible alternative solutions. Be equipped. Be ready. Have some ingenuity. Many times you will find a better plan. Then set out the alternatives with them but not over drinks. Reflect over all that's happened. Having listened to them express their emotions and having stepped into their shoes, you now know how to calm them down.

Sales Practitioner Beware!
Approach with Due Caution

How about another example but with a slightly different twist? You are working for the sellers. You have done your research and are on the job. The prospective buyers ask a question that could potentially be an opportunity for you to be abrupt. Buyers like to ask if the home is furnished. Let's say it's not. I don't just blurt out and say NO.

Why am I so carefully here?

From my experience, I know that although this is a real question, the real concern is uncertain, so behind this question may be another that may truly need to be addressed.

I believe something like this happens at one time or another to most of us if we ever call any 1-800 customer service line. If they haven't been trained to deeply listen, it's painful. They give you an answer before you ask the question. They jump the gun.

So why behave like that phone person when you want to get to the real concern and not alienate them with an answer they don't want and don't need to get? Because as you will see, there are various possibilities. Let's NOW explore the whole truth of the situation and **our** role to play.

In certain market places and many builder models, the home is furnished. It is hard to tell sometimes because on occasion the furniture is placed in the house just to make people see the possibilities for decorating the room but not as permanent fixtures that go with the house.

Some people use asking about the furniture merely as a conversation starter. Some people develop a burning desire for the furniture itself. Some people have a burning desire for a simplified move and want all that in place. Of course some people like the house and are repulsed by the furniture- and/or the picture, and/or the lamps.

So my intention after that question is often to delay an answer and find out the motivation behind that question. I personally want to be an asset to those who come through the listing, which I serve, but in responding to people, I don't want to forget about what I have learned from the hundreds of transactions I have experienced. Keep in mind, although I may circumvent a direct answer at the time, the place in my head is fully committed to serving. The place in my heart is calm with a resolve that I am helpful. I'm a professional. My brand is to be someone they can and will trust.

As I have indicated, true learning experiences have happened because of my relationships during transactions. For instance I've had Grad and Medical students sell all their furniture on Craigslist the week before closing. And then they buy everything on Craigslist when they get to their next University stop. The first time this happened, I was awestruck by their commitment to their goals. When I asked, they told me, "No moving costs, except getting the pets and books into the car for a road trip." The freedom from this expense, I was told, gave them more money for the next phase in their life.

Goals like these are not age or demographic specific. During the real estate depression, sellers of multi-million-dollar short sales did the same thing. They gave everything away they couldn't move in their cars. They believed that the quicker they shed all expense, the quicker they bounced back.

I was inspired by their focus and determination. Paying it forward during these times of transition for the families I have helped has always brought them favor in their future. I'm still in contact with them and see how things have worked out for many of these friends on Facebook.

At our family reunion last year in Iowa, my childhood horse-riding best friend, Susie Lee, had just moved her son Matt from Stanford. *Hey, a truck with a trailer and $250 bucks gets you everything you need to live in Madison!*

What a fun story to share around the picnic table. Susie, being a bi-coastal professional herself, and showing her son how's it done!

Everywhere I go, one of the top five questions I'm asked about my profession involves the execution of moving. It helps me stay grounded on the concerns of the audience I serve. I believe everyone wants to own a home. That's my mindset, positive, truly creative, as it employs an understanding of future generations and the space we need. It's active in the "now." And it's responsive, encompassing the best part of spirit, mind, and soul.

> Let's reflect again for the moment. What are the top priorities expressed in your conversations with clients? Do you really what to know what your clients are asking? Or do you just want to bust out the answer you think they need?

Here is one way to be respectful in this instance, a method I use to listen to the furniture question and find deeper meaning without jumping the gun. I replay to the question with another. I either ask, *"Would you like it to be furnished?"* or, *"Do you need it to be furnished?"*

If they need it to be furnished, and the seller is moving with their stuff, I have top-notch designers who can make it happen on any budget. The Craigslist option is always good in a pinch. And who knows, maybe the seller will change their minds if I ask them to. The extra cash and the unexpected ease of their next move might be too great a temptation for them to pass up.

So on this journey of yeses and nos, which we have embarked on, their can be some valuable surprises and benefits when you begin to see things with consciousness, good intention, and the right way how, when, and why to say NO!

The Limits of Empathy

Whatever tone might be set in transactions, you must set the tone for them to feel to ask questions. Asking doesn't hurt anything. Yes, some of these questions may be overly emotional or illogical. Why are they dealing with issues this way? Maybe you'd like to wrap your head around it, but sometimes you just can't.

Sometimes people are so inwardly confused, it is hard to gauge where they are coming from.

It doesn't always really matter if you can't empathize.

In method acting, the idea is to get into character by virtue of emotional resonances with the characters that you dig up from your own life experience. In continental acting, you relate to the character by emulating his external characteristics, his body gestures, his tone, his accent, his manner of dress, his colloquial expressions.

But some people either are so confused, you can't read them or so duplicitous by nature that they can successfully hide their feelings.

You are not going to get anywhere if they are covertly influenced to hide their concerns. Interactions are better. Let their questions and concerns see the light of day. You get zero from the unrequested question or the unspoken concern.

So to do this, you may have to go with an abstract continental acting style analysis. In this case, you have to figure out what is going on without feeling anything spontaneously sympathetic within yourself. Then you must endeavor to figure out what they truly mean or want from how they act, what they say, and what their body language and address yourself to it, even if you can't really empathize with them in any natural way.

• • • • •

> When has empathy failed to work for you? What did you
> do to handle the situation without feeling any empathy or
> the client or their position?

. . . . .

END NOTES

1. Dr. Caroline Leaf, *Who Switched Off My Brain* (Southlake, Texas: Improv, Ltd., 2009)

Chapter 8

MINDFULNESS
Being There for the Sale
Being There for Yourself

First of all, I am an author who spends most of the day making sales. I love sales, perhaps specifically because I love people and I love helping them find beautiful homes. There is something about real estate that I find exciting, and I find everything about that somewhat demanding sales process intriguing, although often challenging. I like being an expert in my specific field.

Conscious Selling – A New Type of Sales

White Hat Sales is not just a cold, dry collection of techniques designed so that you can exploit and manipulate people. It is a system of interconnected concepts and practices to empower you to transform yourself into a sales practitioner who can actually *Be There For The Sale.*

Being There for the Sale in the sense that I use it involves *conscious selling*, and in many ways, is the opposite of *hypnotic selling*, which is a subset of Black Hat Sales. Hypnotic selling, as described previously, is a form of selling we have seen used as a core element in various variations of NLP selling, and in a sense, is all about putting people to sleep (into at least a light trance). Maybe we could even call it *hypno-gogic selling*. When you are going to sleep but still conscious, you enter into a world mid-way between sleeping and waking. When you are put into a very light trance, you are lulled into a kind of dreamy wakefulness or semi-wakeful dreaminess, a state which enhances suggestibility.

Conscious selling involves practices, particularly like mindfulness, reframing one's approach to life through changing one's inner narratives, eschewing anger and depression by taking 100% responsibility for one's life, trying passionately to help others, submitting oneself to ruthless but benign self-analysis, and other practices that have been developed over millennia by practitioners in many faith-based religions, spiritual organizations, movements, and literature of very diverse points of views and practices, modern psychological schools, and disciplines and the findings of neuroscience.

• • • • •

How would you describe conscious selling? In what ways has your approach to selling mirrored some of the techniques or ideas of conscious selling? What is the difference between conscious selling and hypnotic selling?

• • • • •

Mindfulness is an extremely old practice. It is a route to self-awareness by which I mean awareness of yourself in the present moment in ordinary life, but it is also a means to become closer and even connect to your Divine Self.

We believe that many of these practices, regardless of what organization or individual expresses them, is somewhat embodied in nature itself, which itself is embodied in a greater consciousness.

Whereas we do not wish to get deeply into theology, we could point that conventional theology often says that God is both immanent and transcendent in Creation. This means that He is embodied in physical reality and is above it.

To make a comparison between immanence and transcendence in relation to human consciousness, one can imagine paying attention to one's legs when one is doing some simple leg squats. We always have the ability to become conscious of much of our physical functionality, which if you think about, has a consciousness of their own. For instance we might say, "My leg hurts" or "My feet are getting warmer," as though they are conscious of pain or warmth on their own that feeling pain or warmth is immanent in their nature, in their capacity to experience these things.

Yet when one is thinking about sailing over the weekend or going to a movie that one has been looking forward to for months, while one is doing leg squats, one can forget about the consciousness of pain in one's upper thighs for a moment. Although the sense receptors of our body may be affected by our imagination (such as certain visualization exercises performed by athletes), the effects are not quite the same. Less distinct.

But if after focusing on your imagination about the future, then you decide to pay attention to the present moment, you notice the pain is there. The "I" that then becomes the witness of that pain that the leg is experiencing is transcendent of that pain. It is above that pain and can leave it and attend to other things. So in a sense, human consciousness, in the form of the consciousness inherent in the body, and in the form of consciousness outside the body and the physical realm of these organs or parts of the body, is transcendent of them.

The body feels pain, but the witness to the pain, the consciousness is above that pain.

In some fashion, the experiential reality which connects man's consciousness to the core of the universe, to the consciousness of God is connected to that sense of "I" that connects the human consciousness with his own body but also transcends it.

Immanence means, for want of a better way of expressing it, consciousness within manifested reality. Consistent but opposite with this concept of immanence, transcendence means consciousness apart from manifested reality. God is transcendent and immanent in respect to all of manifested reality. Your mind, apart from discussing its connection to Divine Reality, is transcendent from manifested reality and also very immanent, intrinsically involved in everything you think and do in the world you navigate through every day.

That's all very well, but the connection between your reality and the reality of God in human consciousness is extraordinarily important.

The connection between human and divine consciousness, as discussed previously, has I imagine, many different levels, both conscious and unconscious. On the highest level, I believe human consciousness gives way to the Presence of the Divine. On the level of human consciousness in what I would call the "soul" level, our consciousness partakes of the Divine Presence, we may be a drop in the ocean but is a Divine Ocean. Still our connectedness to our divine nature gives us the possibility of a whole different way of living as a human being. Although I am seriously opting for humility, I would not want to put any limits on the possibility of deeper and deeper with the Divine Presence. But one should clearly say here that although our souls can consciously partake of the Presence of God, there is for some who at least theoretically know about their divine nature, a danger to believe that somehow their lower nature, their very flawed and human ego, is the Divine Nature. While this is often the stuff of psychosis, there is a subtle type of egotism and self-aggrandizement that is one of the worst of human beings fatal flaws, mistaking their own lower personality, their altogether too-human ego as being divine. The Roman Emperors, who appointed themselves as gods, readily partook of this self-deception.

But to those who truly know the Divine Presence, it is a sense of "I" filled with love and light, not the strutting, manipulative, and controlling sense of superiority of the human ego. This is not to say that those who understand and know about states of consciousness inherent in this Presence don't experience a sense of empowerment unique to this important component of human experience.

If this transcendent "I" in man is connected to God, can it also have a creative power, perhaps as some have alleged to change the physical world. For quite some time, in the modern world, many writers and speakers have alleged that conception, recently connecting the capacity of thought to change physical reality to quantum physics. Recently this became a very popular conception owing to the success of the book and video, *The Secret*, but the fact is this idea of "manifestation," the ability to manifest what is in one's thought in the physical world is inherent in the New Testament, in teachings such as that of Louise Hay and Wayne Dyer, who followed such teachers as Earl Nightingale or Napoleon Hill.

It is also manifest in certain elements of Christian evangelism, such as those who believe in "name it and claim it." Whether these teachings are pure or distorted is beyond the scope of this book, except to say we believe there is something to these ideas and we plan to connect the idea of *conscious selling* to the true self-awareness and the alignment of our thoughts to the greater good inherent in the proper understanding of the nature of things.

One caveat, which will mention but not fully explicate, is our belief that consciousness of Self, the "I" that can imagine a different world or a different time or experience pain in one's leg or a cool breeze on one's face may ultimately be connected to our Source, but it is not quite the same consciousness. That consciousness of the Divine Presence or the Spirit of God is a further refinement of ordinary consciousness, a higher frequency some would say, and is the place within ourselves which is the depositary of our true nature, our true desires, and the capacity to connect them to the real world.

As I indicated, some authors, sometimes scientifically trained or scientific professionals, theorists believe that this understanding is beginning to be touched by such scientific disciplines as quantum mechanics but also by biofeedback, MRIs, and other physiological methods of measurement and various types of cognitive psychology, which demonstrates that human thought can be a discreet and measurable neurological event.

One of my favorite researchers on this subject, Carolyn Leaf, gave a Ted talk on March 16th, 2015.[1] Carolyn was a therapist in the 1980's long before the concept of neuroplasticity was proven or even a rational topic of discussion in the scientific community. I would say that her instinct for the belief that the brain can be altered by the mind, at a time when brain damage was considered virtually incapable of significant repair, demonstrates how Spirit and human invention, discovery, and innovation can be connected.

For a therapist at that time to pursue the quixotic concept of mind over brain matter was both risky, career-wise, and counter-intuitive, scientifically, yet her results were startling to say the least. She quickly moved from measurable success in one-to-one therapy to becoming a teacher of teachers whose discipline of transmitting techniques of deep thinking and concentrated focus worked wonders with victims of serious accidents, PTSD, and learning disabilities. Science has now become the handmaiden of Leaf and other's divine inspiration.

Much of the material in this book is predicated on the ability of the human personality to make extraordinary changes. Although I believe this information can help effect transformation in many different professions, and as Carolyn Leaf points out, science is quickly coming to fully prove a point of view which was considered ridiculous (the name of her Ted Talk) just three or four decades ago.

I see successful salespeople actively living this new reality by using their mind to actively change their brains and help others around them grow. Truly creative activities from a loving Creator giving us the same ability.

In Whose Image?
Unveiling the Goodness Within

In the way we are speaking of mindfulness in this chapter, we are speaking of being mindful of ourselves, in the present moment, but also mindful of our principles and goals inherent in our thoughts and manifest in our behavior. Again we believe that this awareness connects us more directly with Source than an "ordinary" state of consciousness, but perhaps this is only the first level of this connection and there are enhanced possibilities for experiencing this connection more fully. Many of the ramifications of this connection are beyond this book.

Suffice to say if we realize that the Source of all things is purely good, then we realize that our true direction, our real vocation partakes of that goodness, and that our goals and our thoughts must be aligned with the demands of that sacred journey to perfect that reality in our lives. It is important therefore, since none of us are perfect, that the journey of self-examination is critical if we are going to stay on the White Hat path.

Mindfulness, in the sense of being aware of the present moment of our mind, body, and thoughts, is therefore a critical part of empowering oneself. It is also, I believe, a ladder to greater self-awareness.

For that reason, we believe that everyone who wishes, from many varying points of view to become a *sales practitioner,* must commit themselves to many of the core elements of mindfulness embedded in the White Hat methodology to further enhance their relationship between their profession and their true, deepest desires, which ultimately connect themselves to Source. As I mentioned earlier, I believe that commerce, trading goods/services for goods/services, is a natural part of man's nature and in a certain way connected to the world of nature manifesting around us. As creatures created in God's image, our potential is to fully partake of the good, of divine love, and therefore we do not ideally partake of the predatory instincts of certain components of the natural world. We are not talking about self-defense but rather the desire to kill and conquer based on greed, selfishness, and the joy of hurting.

So let us say I see the desire to be involved in White Hat Sales as potentially a very strong desire for someone in the field of sales who wishes to manifest to the best of his or her ability. This then would require a commitment to an effective alliance with the Source behind all things.

And why not? If indeed IN GOD WE TRUST.

> **Do you believe that human consciousness is somehow connected to core of the universe, to the consciousness of God?**

• • • • •

White Hat Sales
A Route to Becoming the Person You Really Are

I have developed this paradigm to that interested readers, like yourself, can become the person you really are and find the highest level of gratification in human life possible for someone involved in sales transactions. In this manner, White Hat Sales will allow you to both others and serve the divine nature within yourself, which is so intimately connected to the Source of all things. This, I believe, is the real meaning of self-fulfillment in a professional and vocational sense.

• • • • •

> **Do you feel you have a mission? If so describe it succinctly but carefully.**

• • • • •

No system or process created to aid you in your personal development can truly function without your deep reflection, your careful discrimination, your agreement, and your commitment.

No one is asking you to agree with everything I say or with every detail of this process. Like me you need to come to terms with what you believe and what works for you.

But I can tell you, in my mind, every technique and process mentioned in this book is interconnected. Still the fact that I believe that does not give you some kind of free license to believe it. You need to make up your mind. Ultimately you will build your specific sales process out of many different factors and experiences in your life. White Hat Sales is a process I am designing and will continue to design. It is not a meant to be a gospel of final truth but a route to self-knowledge designed by another human like yourself. I doubt if any other designer of a sales system can say much more.

• • • • •

> **Does taking on the White Hat Sales path denote a total commitment to everything in the book or described in any literature about this profit?**

• • • • •

In this book, I am providing you with a paradigm of a different kind of sales process, what I liked to call conscious selling. This involves a certain way of life, a certain perspective and some very specific focus on what is real and what is important.

Just like method acting, in the minds of some of the greatest actors of the last century,helped actors forge characters out of the deep recesses of their minds, White Hat Sales will make you dig deep into yourself to bring out the wonderful treasures of life that emerge when you begin to truly know yourself, a foundation that will help you to truly align yourself with Spirit.

• • • • •

> Given the intention and the methodology, do you think that White Hat Sales might help you become a better person, as well as a more competent and successful sales person?

• • • • •

Living in the Moment

A few years ago, Janice Maturano, the founder of an institute for training corporate management, wrote a book called *Finding the Space to Lead: A Practical Guide to Mindful Leadership.*[2] Maturino was, at one time, the Vice President of Public Responsibility and Deputy General Counsel, General Mills Inc. Maturano's technique was a based on a spiritual practice thousands of years old, but she brought it specifically into the corporate world and explored some of its applications to management, eventually breaking off from General Mills to found her own institute to teach mindful leadership.

Being mindful means being aware of yourself in the present moment. In psychological programs like A.C.T., it means observing yourself under many conditions in daily living often, as in their anger management techniques, learning when or when not to express what you observe. In other types of programs, it may be helpful mean observing and identifying destructive or counter productive self-talk and then formulating new narratives or affirmations to counteract subconscious negativities. Being mindful during the sales process can heighten awareness of the agent, buyer, or seller, provide body language, tones of voice, and facial expression clues to hidden narratives and positive, progressive interest in various parts of the process, leading to more wisdom in understanding the client's point of view and needs. Perhaps more importantly, mindfulness can also give you a greater clue as to what is going on in yourself.

You can call White Hat Sales a form of conscious selling based on bearing down on each situation and relationship with a very powerful sense of presence. "Presence" means that you are aligned with purpose in the context of mind, body, and spirit very much rooted in the present moment, where the senses of hearing, taste, vision, and touch are awakened while the interactions with your clients or while doing paperwork or when chatting on the phone with a vendor are vibrantly alive through an effort of will.

Being mindful means paying attention to what you are doing on many levels. At the highest level, it means being aware of your physical body, feelings, thought, sensations, and moreover, at the highest levels, even awareness itself. You could say that paying attention is the main foundation of mindfulness.

Martina Sheehan and Susan Pearse, who have written a book called *One Moment Please: It's Time to Pay Attention*, have written this marvelous homage to this extraordinary faculty of human consciousness.

> Attention is as real and tangible as the light that surrounds you and the gravity that holds you in place. It is a physical force, mysterious but familiar nevertheless. You know when you are in its presence, and you know when it is being withheld from you. You know when your attention is stable and healthy, and

> you know when it is stretched and strained… Attention is a birthright to be honored, precious but more fragile than we have ever realized.[3]

Let us imagine a situation with a client in which you are discussing their purchase of a home, an event which occurs to me often more than several times in a week.

In this conversation, you pay attention to the client, but you are also aware of the hum of the air conditioner, the feel of the cool air on your hands and arms, the smell of fresh paint on the walls of the room, the tension in your shoulders when the client relates his discomfort with his present home and the dishonest way it was sold to him, all the while as you are paying close attention to your client's every word while closely watching his gestures and body language.

By paying attention to the sights and sounds around you, those elements of experience, which we often regard as somehow subsidiary to our important moments of business, *we root ourselves in the present moment*, which once understood and accomplished, actually enhances our effectiveness in interactions with other people and the world. In a certain way, we become a sales practitioner at least partially formed in the like of a Sherlock Holmes, able to perceive relatively minute details around us and catch things in the body language, tonality, and words of our client that can help produce more meaningful interactions.

Although it is important to be able to more completely assess your client's state of mind to help guide him to the right decisions, it is far more important to use mindfulness to observe yourself.

By using mindfulness in this way, life does indeed become a daily personal growth experience, a growth in the ability to communicate, to organize better what you are going to say, to articulate yourself clearly when you do, to say things that you have sufficiently reflected on and to withhold those feelings and thoughts that may pass through your mind but reflect unnecessary anger, disappointment, resentment, or even retaliation and revenge for someone's aggressive behavior against you. It should be clear to anyone who knows themselves that this type of inner work is difficult and takes much attention, cautiousness, dedication, and knowledge to proceed with successfully.

Mindfulness and Alignment
Point of Contact with the Divine

Besides the use of mindfulness to be more able to choose reflectiveness over spontaneous, injurious, or premature reflexibility, there is another most important component to this process- *alignment*.

Whereas this is a very important concept, we can only begin to address what this means in this relatively short book, and the scope of this subject surely exceeds its application to the sales process.

Alignment means connecting your conscious thoughts and feelings, and their expression to your true sense of mission in your vocation and your life.

How do we know what our mission is? I think the best clue in our ordinary state of consciousness is by a vital feeling for what we are or wish to be engaged in, a passion that we cannot ignore.

I think that Megan Dalla-Camina, a business strategist that is also a motivational speaker and consultant, has written very precisely about this quality of human psychology and its powerful influence on our inner direction. As she writes in *Getting Real About Having it All*:

> Our passions define us, they tell the world who we are, and what we care about, and they can make the difference between a life just lived, or a life fulfilled. Our passions ignite us, they get the fire burning somewhat; deep down in our souls, and they make us want to leap out of bed in the morning and stay up all night. They make us come alive.[4]

Anyone who knows themselves, regardless of their ideal vision of themselves, knows they are self-divided in various ways. As Paul says in Romans 7:15, *"For that which I do I allow not: for what I would, that do I not; but what I hate, that do I."*

What Paul is speaking, here is something most people can easily see about themselves. For instance you apply for a job. In the past, you have said to yourself perhaps not as formally as in the following statement but essentially, though wordlessly, within yourself. We are assuming in this example you are an IT professional.

> *I believe in my abilities and I believe that, with persist-ence, I can get the IT management job I have always hoped for. So I promise myself that I will unwaveringly commit myself to this next job search.*

The foregoing is a good rendering of a commitment based on a person involved in the profession of Information Technology and wishing to secure permanent employment in that area.

Imagine now, after a record-breaking five interviews in various tiers of a well-paying, highly respected international IT company, he is ultimately rejected.

Three minutes after receiving the news, the applicant becomes very depressed and angry, saying in effect:

> *Those idiots. I spent hours studying how to present the cut-ting edge work I did for _____ (his or her last com-pany)…and they just didn't get it. I could tell just from the questions they asked me afterwards, that the lead in-terviewer, the so-called head of their stupid IT department, did not have a clue as to what I was talking about, which means he is running his department five years behind ev-eryone else. Still they are known as leaders in IT applica-tions to oil companies, which is exactly where I belong. But*

if I can't get through to them, who should know their
stuff, why should I be able to get anywhere? I'm totally
screwed. Maybe I should take that Personnel Manage-
ment position that my aunt offered me, even though I
hate even the thought of it.

Although that type of narrative may seem rather long, it is only one
example of many lengthy narratives or even full-fledged dramatic and
fully-imagined scenarios, sometimes with dialogue and action, just
like a movie that can play out in our minds after a disappointment in
getting a job, in a love relationship, in a failure to be elected, to be
promoted, to easily fix a lawnmower, or to be successful in an important sales transaction.

. . . . .

**How do you react when your mission seems to be frus-
trated by repetitive delays and obstacles? Is there a point
where your whole psyche seems to become totally toxic?
Do you ever enter the realm of complete depression and
hopefulness? If you did long-term or short-term, how did
you combat it? Ultimately did you bring these feelings
under control? If so, how?**

. . . . .

Like Paul you may note that this is the kind of self-contradiction of
one's intent, mission, and commitment that you have clearly professed
to yourself, but that doesn't mean you can stop it. You may try but,
"For that which I do, I allow not," which probably means in more contemporary language, *"For that which I would do, I do not allow."*

In other words, you may want to stop that long narrative or inner action movie, but you don't seem to be able to. It keeps playing out in your mind, sometimes ad infinitum.

But being ambivalent about a new job or new position is not unusual. What is odd is how little people realize how much they are divided within about this kind of situation and thousands of others. It just isn't all that easy being a human being.

And we sales practitioners are human beings, aren't we?

· · · · ·

Do you agree that most people have a great deal of self-division? How would you describe three areas in which you seem to be divided within yourself?

· · · · ·

I cannot tell you that there is just one way to stop that narrative in your mind. But one passage from Dr. Wayne Dyer's amazing autobiography, *I Can See Clearly Now*[5], truly seems a way, one that needs work to attain though, for sure.

In his book, he notes that "fear is a mental exercise that's a habitual response lodged in the subconscious mind from early childhood that arises when we anticipate the unknown. He further says that "love is what's left when I let go of fear."[6]

· · · · ·

In terms of self-division, what value is there knowing that fear and love are incompatible?

. . . . .

In the example above, after the job rejection, obviously the applicant in their long harangue about their bleak future and why don't they just stop trying and take a lesser job, the potential decision is motivated by fear of the future, not the wonderful *perfect IT job dream* they may have been saying to themselves as they climbed up the ladder of IT experience and professionalism. Since the first narrative, hypothetically, was their long-held sense of their vocation and therefore one of the main wishes for their future, the second narrative was definitely not aligned with that dream.

This does not mean that along the way to a perfect dream, there aren't stages, in this case lesser job or activities, but taking them means you are willing to work towards your dream, not kick over the ladder so there is no way ever of accomplishing your goals.

. . . . .

Perhaps of all the concepts we have presented, alignment is the most significant. After reading this, or through your own thoughts and research, how do you interpret the meaning of alignment?

. . . . .

The attempt to align myself with the Divine Nature is part of my life, an exciting practical reality. But like all those who are willing to make that attempt, there are obstacles.

As Wayne Dyer says further as to changing his negative narratives:

> When a push-pull comes up that involves indecision and doubt, I remind myself that the anxiety is an emotional response, and therefore it must be coming from either love or fear, and since love is not stressful, it must be a fear that is at play. I then simply go to a loving place within, and the indecision is resolved. I find that if I let myself get quiet and meditate on the issue, the loving guidance shows up...[7]

There are many ways to transform yourself, but when you can find that place Wayne Dyer calls that "loving place within,"[8] you have graduated from jet speed to a starship's faster-than-light hyperdrive.

· · · · ·

Do you have a "loving place within?"

· · · · ·

END NOTES

1.   Dr. Caroline Leaf, "Ridiculous" (YouTube Video), March 16, 2015 https://www.youtube.com/watch?v=yjhANyrKpv8

2. Janice Maturano, *Finding the Space to Lead: A Practical Guide to Mindful Leadership* (New York: Bloomsbury Press, 2014)

3. Martina Sheehan and Susan Pearse, *One Moment Please: It's Time to Pay Attention* (Carlsbad, California: Hay House, 2015), 3

4. Megan Dalla-Camina, *Getting Real About Having it All* (Carlsbad, California: Hay House, 2012), 3

5. Wayne Dyer, *I Can See Clearly Now*, (Carlsbad, California: Hay House, 2012)

6. Ibid.

7. Ibid.

8. Ibid.

Chapter 9

CREATING NEW INNER NARRATIVES
KEYS TO SELF-TRANSFORMATION

Changing your inner narratives is no easy thing, and whereas we are addressing it in this book, a great deal of work and study is needed to make dramatic and continual change.

Human behavior is derived from conscious and unconscious narratives but probably also from long-term, habitual, spontaneous responses that may not be easily connected to descriptive narratives. But even these spontaneous responses can often analyze and converte to narratives for the purpose of self-examination and self-correction.

Our Best Response

Our best response to people demands a cool, kind, and responsive demeanor. This kind of demeanor enhances success in every area of human contact.

For almost every person who ever needed a job, the primary and continual form of sales is, as in that job-hunting effort, selling themselves. But a job search is often very difficult, time-consuming, and disappointing. When facing a panel or sequence of interviewers, the need for avoiding any extreme reaction, like depression or anger, from a strong no is paramount.

• • • • •

In what ways have you conducted a job hunt? Did you find this more difficult than selling a service or a product to others, that is when your personal fate was so much involved? Give a few examples how you handled a no.

• • • • •

The importance of creating the right personal connection is demonstrated by Granovetter's 1974 study of how to get a job. In this study, Granovetter demonstrated how jobs are secured mainly by networking, during a time when the Internet did not even exist. His study showed how "formal application," for instance applying to classified advertising, using employment agencies or placement agencies in universities or professional associations that promoted specific jobs was accounting for less than 20% of acquiring successful employment. On the other hand, an equal amount was through direct application by the person going directly to a company, which had not advertised. The rest was through personal contacts who informed or even assisted people in getting their jobs. Basically through networking.[1]

• • • • •

According to Granovetter, what is the best process to get a job? Why is that way so superior? Will it work now?

• • • • •

Narratives within yourself that blow up your self-importance, that harbor and produce immediate negativity when your point of view has been challenged, that reinforce the idea of retaliation for any supposed slight by another person, that produce great anxiety when any kind of change in economic or social position is necessitated are all narratives that must be examined.

• • • • •

> **Besides those mentioned above, what other kind of spontaneous negative narratives can keep you from responding correctly?**

• • • • •

How can one change these types of reactions?

First, perhaps you must make a decision. Are people essentially good but make the wrong choices? Or are they essentially unredeemable and bad?

Whereas anything I might say about narratives might have to be highly customized to be applicable to an individual, I will risk some general thoughts about what causes, say strong negativity or even violence, verbally or physically against another person when they have been deeply insulted by another person.

Let's say you have been fired? Do you say:

> _____ *is the stupidest person I have ever met. I'd really like to deck him out. Imagine I go to all this trouble*

*to create an almost perfect inventory system and one,
just one stupid clerk makes a simple mistaken and that
idiot takes me in front of the entire sale and tells them
what an idiot I am. So I called him what he is, a stupid
son of a bitch, and after five years as the best grocery
manager in the entire region, he fires me on the spot.
I'm just sorry I didn't walk up to him and punch him
in the face.*

I grant you that most of the people reading this would never say that
to a boss. But I will also speculate that many reading this book might
say it to themselves and fantasize about a related incident, and that
might affect their demeanor and attitude towards being publicly crit-
icized even if they remain silent.

• • • • •

> **Give an example of a reflexive reaction that occurred to
> you when you were laid off or fire or just lost your temper
> with your boss or upper management.**

• • • • •

Is that inner, boiling anger inside necessary? What is behind it? Can
it be stopped?

Let us take a look at some sayings in the Old Testament and Gospels from a psychological perspective.

I would say that when insulted like this, the most common reflexive reaction is "an eye for an eye and a tooth for a tooth." In this case,
it is not a form of future punishment but a justification for punishment

right now, either verbally or physically. The narrative justification that might be constructed to represent this response might be:

If a person unjustly attacks me in any way, he deserves immediate and profound retaliation on the level of his attack.

Another point about what is behind this narration is the concept of an enemy or a criminal who has no real human value, does not deserve empathy, and deserves to be hurt or destroyed. Believe it or not, even people in close relationships or even a long-term marriage, when in the grips of reflexive anger, can in a split second, categorize their friend or beloved on verbally into an enemy. This is a form of depersonalization that justifies verbal or physical violence. Besides being a common destructive element in relationships, it also can be a long-standing emotional point of view that can cause and perpetuate war between nations.

When you depersonalize a person or a country, you leave off the kind of restraints you would deploy in naturally dealing with people. You are willing to kill or maim in war. In personal fights, you are willing to maim emotionally at the very least.

· · · · ·

Do you ever have an incident that makes you turn a friend, loved one, or associate to an actual enemy in your thinking and imagination? Have you ever taken these feelings into the real world and made your home or business a place of physical or verbal combat?

· · · · ·

Looking at the news, it does not take much ingenuity to realize that much of humanity seems to believe such things and that they also pass the blame onto the family of their enemies and perhaps their neighbors, their religious colleagues, their ethnicity, and their country. And they are willing to take offensive and even lethal actions at individuals and all those they think are associated with them.

· · · · ·

> In your life and experience, what kind of spontaneous negative narratives can keep you from responding correctly to the challenges presented in sales or personal relationships? Are they similar or different?

· · · · ·

I presume though that most of my readers here are more concerned with individuals who have taken unfair action against them in the sales process. As an example, it could very well be a person who has accepted and used a product or service and then suddenly has second thoughts about it and tries, perhaps unscrupulously, to get their money back, perhaps leveling false accusations against the seller.

Still many of my readers may feel, on a daily basis, anger against clients, relatives, former friends, professional colleagues who they feel may have abused them. And many of you who experience either a mild, medium, or viral form of this anger may regret this experience for a number of reasons.

For one thing, recurring anger like this robs one of the joy of life and therefore interferes with one's relations with others, even those who are not a party to any overt or external action based on the anger.

Still the extreme drain on one's psyche occurs because the anger itself creates continual sadness, depression, or abstraction from the environment what might appear to others as a bad mood. It does not help one to be responsive or benevolent to those colleagues, friends, or clients around one.

. . . . .

> **Be honest. Is anger a problem for you?**
> **How big a problem?**

. . . . .

Besides these problems, recurring anger often profoundly sets off an escalating chain reaction between the offended and the offender, who probably thought they had a good reason for the attack in the first place.

. . . . .

> **Give an example of a way you treated a customer reflexively and in a negative way and what you did to reverse the bad effects of what you did with the client or in the future.**

. . . . .

How do you neutralize such inward thoughts?

First of all, you might question the utility of "an eye for an eye" as a maxim for behavior and then perhaps jump to the controversial command in the Gospels or various other sacred or personal development literature, which states, "Love your enemy."

Transforming Toxic Anger

If you were that star grocery manager and had been publicly humiliated because of perhaps a new and inexperienced clerk who couldn't follow orders but did not want to experience that level of anger, what are your alternatives?

· · · · ·

> **What kind of narratives do you think is running through your unconscious when you get angry? Give concrete examples based on actual events.**

· · · · ·

I would say that brainstorming and choosing alternative responses couldn't take place in the midst of a confrontation permeated with anger. It would probably have taken an earlier former commitment to a different kind of narrative about getting along with difficult people. Not just a commitment but rehearsal and practice in the real world. Perhaps a more positive narrative might go something like this:

> *I realize that every person has a core or goodness within*
> *them, no matter how they think, speak, or act. For that*
> *reason, I will seek inwardly to connect with that core of*
> *goodness with a person that probably will, is, or has of-*

fended me through my imagination. Even if I need to protect myself physically, I will hold onto that feeling of caring and love that comes when I feel that goodness in another person.

But to say constructing a narrative like this will produce change is an understatement. The subconscious is a mighty power within ourselves that takes considerable effort to gain control over and has a tremendous influence on our lives.

White Hat Sales depends on developing and following certain protocols in your life portfolio, but inner transformation is one of them that needs to be highly under your control and be customized to you by you as exactly as possible.

Tools for Transformation

Books

Reading books on personal development is important. I am not going to recommend any books in this section but rather explain why they are important.

Both self-correction of one's demeanor and actions in the world are manifestations of accurate methods and theories of self-transformation and involve creating dominant thought in the conscious mind that can be eventually transferred to the subconscious mind, over-ruling negative and self-destructive subconscious narratives.

Although this is critical to White Hat Sales practitioners just for their performance, it is also critical for them to achieve both their business and personal goals.

• • • • •

> **Do you read salesmanship, motivational, or business books for the purpose of enhancing your sales activities? What are your favorite books in these genres?**

• • • • •

Although saying *you are your thoughts* is a bit of a cliché and over-simplification, there is a great truth in that. Perhaps it is more accurate to say that your thoughts influence your life in a much more direct way than you might think.

This is not just an academic issue for me. I have witnessed in my own life many concrete demonstrations that the words we speak, backed by the beliefs we hold, create energy that brings events together.

Thirty-three-year-old Thomas Jefferson was not aiming at originality by articulating the highest ideals of the American Revolution, liberty, equality, and the right to self-determination by the American at that time, as we have now, clearly embraced a view of the world that postulated that a person's position is determined, not by birth, rank, or title but by talent, ability, and enterprise.

My view and experience are right in line with the people who founded our country, that we are all created equal and endowed by our Creator with certain unalienable Rights, that among these are life, liberty, and the pursuit of happiness.

Consider for a moment what a momentous moment that was, what an extraordinary change in the governmental structure in the world at that time, populated by kings and lords, an aristocracy of blood, not ability, maintaining its power by force and not by the will of the people. How amazing were the events that led to the writing of the Declaration and the unlikely and difficult revolution that stood up against one of the greatest military organizations in the world at that time.

I believe that although we have freedom of choice, the choices that align with the will of God have a strange, miraculous priority in the world of manifestation.

And for millennia, until that time, the rule of monarchs was not an expression of the true desire of the people of those manifold counties but perhaps they lacked the heart and soul, the primordial conviction and spiritual power of our Founding Fathers.

But once the wish was finally formulated by those aligned with the Divine Presence, men like Jefferson, Washington, Madison, Franklin, and so many others, then manifestation was possible. By writing, speaking, and living the freedom, goals and purposes so articulated in the Declaration, the groundwork for dramatic manifestation was securely laid.

But manifestation requires more than simply belief. It requires the ability to get divine guidance from within and then to take concrete immediate action. What we think, what we believe, what we speak, and the actions to make it happen makes it come to pass. That the manifestation of freedom is still enjoyed 200 years later is evidence of a big vision from a unified vision, enjoyed by men who undoubtedly share the best hopes for humanity bit a benevolent Creator.

> The First Continental Congress represented different interests, religions, and regions; they held conflicting opinions as to how best to restore their rights. The fifty-four men who composed this group did not all know each other; some did not even like each other. With no history of successful cooperation, they struggled to overcome their differences and without any way of knowing if the future held success or nooses for them all. So if they failed, they faced death sooner than later. If you fail, what are you facing? If you succeed, what are you gaining?

. . . . .

If thinking can actually be a component in *manifestation* (in this case what happens to us in the physical world), then we should be concerned about everything we think.

After studying and applying what our Founders did, I truly believe that there is a great deal to their hypothesis, that our thoughts influence reality.

. . . . .

If your thinking has ever improved in a dramatic and meaningful way, please describe it Do you believe your thoughts actually effect the reality of your life?

. . . . .

By being mindful of our thoughts, we can begin to change them and perhaps see deeper and better things in our lives.

Perhaps we should begin by truly assessing what we have created in our lives so far.

. . . . .

How can books improve the quality of your thinking that could lead to better sales? Why is that important? Why are they such good tools to serve in that direction?

. . . . .

Manifesting What We Actually Want

As I am sanguine in most social situations, most people would not realize that my inner thought life is as serious as it is.

During the time I spent in my first basketball camp, I spent every waking, non-playing hour reading James Michener's *Afghanistan*. This was my first attempt to peer beyond the small world of Iowa into a larger, more complex world with people and places quite different than I knew since childhood.

Now I am a serious person with a serious job. And although I take my profession seriously, I take a look at the rest of my life, including times for fun as time worth using wisely.

Anyone can go to a restaurant, but are you choosing ones you really like? Anyone can go on a vacation, but is this the vacation you really want and have done whatever is necessarily to thoroughly plan it out?

The same goes for friends and family. Are the people you are hanging around with adding to your progression as a person? Are your friends just about a bunch of chatter and useless gossip, or are they people concerned about ideas, about important personal goals, about their community, and about the world?

Are your friends helping you move forward, and are you capable of helping them? Activity does not represent progress. Ask a caterpillar circling in a flowerpot. Going around and around does not get you closer to the garden outside. Even if you speed up.

DISCERNMENT

The human psyche is capable of wanting a great deal of things. People want great cars, great houses, great technology, great relationships, great jobs, etc., but they also can conceivably want to perform the world's greatest bank heist, kidnapping innocent people, and wantonly destroying businesses, so they can steal merchandise during a riot.

So wanting something is not necessarily good.

The more you rise on your own personal spiritual ladder within yourself, the more important that whatever you decide to focus on, in the manner described by our First Continental Congress, should be aligned with that part of you that is a component of your essential nature or spirit or divine nature which is aligned our Creator.

• • • • •

> **When it comes to manifesting what one truly wants, why is discernment so important?**

• • • • •

In his book, *The Spontaneous Healing of Belief: Shattering the Paradigm of False Limits*,[2] Gregg Braden, speaks of how when we are born, all of humanity are born with the gift of being able "to the power to translate the possibilities of our minds into the reality of our world."

But for most of us, this power lies dormant until we change some of our core beliefs about our helplessness in the face of the universe. But when we change our paradigm, then something magical but somehow totally conforming to the hidden reality of our universe begins to happen.

> To fully awaken to our power, however, requires a subtle change in the way we think of our ourselves in life, a shift in belief. Just the way sound creates visible waves as it travels through a droplet of water, our "belief waves" ripple through the quantum fabric of the universe to become our bodies and the healing, abundance, and peace—or disease, lack, and

suffering—that we experience in life. And just the way we can tune a sound to change its patterns, we can tune our beliefs to preserve or destroy all that we cherish, including life itself.[3]

Within a positive connection to this universe of possibilities is the guidance you need to discern what you want, and this connection has many levels, one of which is based on the strong feeling within yourself that you have a mission or purpose whose definition, particularly in relationship to White Hat Sales, must be good for you but also good for the world, your neighbors, your friends, your associates, your city, your country, everything out there.

· · · · ·

> **What does Greg Braden mean when he says we are born with the gift of being able "to the power to translate the possibilities of our minds into the reality of our world?"**

· · · · ·

Obviously some of the things you want will not really affect much outside of your family and your business, but they must be genuinely good.

One method of discerning the difference between a real goal and one coming from one's lower personality is to actually pray about it.

What Goals Should I Focus On?

Your real ones. But how do you tell?

As I mentioned before, it is important to do an assessment of what you actually have at present and see if any of that conforms to your true, inner desires. If it does not, for instance if you are living in a house or apartment that does not fulfill your inner vision, then you will need to envision your dream house.

If you envision something for yourself, it does not have to conform to your present situation financially. It can be very expensive, very rare, very different from anything you have had before, but it must really feel right, something that feels spiritually good, if you like.

It is difficult to describe this feeling in words, but it is something like this is what the universe wants to bring me, this conforms to the divine desire within, this is acceptable to the God that I trust and believe in.

There are many ways of formulating this feeling, but it contains both limitless possibilities of God's generosity, but it also contains the limitations of one's own personal vision of what one wants and a sense of one's comfortableness with that request. Manifestation is partially driven by the strength and genuineness of your desires.

· · · · ·

In what sense can we tell if our desires connect to God's desires for us?

· · · · ·

At this point, one thing should be clear, whereas there are many stages sometimes in the achievement of a certain goal, the end vision is very important and is something to cling to when obstacles and challenges come up. Allow me to go into this further.

· · · · ·

> **Why is it so important to focus on what you have and decide if that is what you really want?**

· · · · ·

Goal-Setting

Setting your goals are important, but the main focus in your imagination, in my opinion, should always be the final state of whatever main goal you are concentrating on. Of course any goal has many stages. The achievement of the final goal is the anchor in your mindset, the reality within that you return to when you are moving towards your goal but are beset with challenges.

At the time of the first Presidential election in 1789, only six percent of the population, that is white, male property owners were eligible to vote. The Fifteenth Amendment extended the right to vote to former male slaves in 1870. American Indians gained the vote under a law passed by Congress in 1924, and women gained the vote with the ratification of the Nineteenth Amendment in 1920.

Since Adam and Eve, women have had equal spiritual power with men endowed from our Creator. But for less than 100 years have women secured the blessings of liberty in the market place. And oh, boy! (ironic expression) have we caught up!

In the salesperson's life, there is NO glass ceiling. There is only self-limitation. Take it from Susan B. Anthony. After casting her ballot in the 1872 election in her hometown of Rochester, New York, she was arrested, indicted, tried, and convicted for voting illegally. At her two-day trial in June 1873, which she described as "the greatest judicial outrage history has ever recorded," she was convicted and sentenced to pay a fine of $100 and court costs. She then took advantage of the high-profile case to promote the cause of woman suffrage. Imagine what she could have done with a YouTube video!

Susan B. Anthony exemplified the primary use of our voice is to create our environment instead of simply just complaining about our environment.

. . . . .

There are many stages in fulfilling a goal. Why is focusing on the ultimate objective so important? If Susan B. Anthony were coaching you today, how would you see your struggle as a potential opportunity for success and change?

. . . . .

There are many ways of formally setting your goals, the simplest being writing them down, sometimes in a separate notebook or in a certain document file. Some people probably keep most of this in their heads.

. . . . .

Name three of your major life goals, related to relationships, business, travel, athletic performance, etc.?

. . . . .

But things get complex because most people have many main goals.

One of the methods for doing this is a vision board, where you draw or assemble pictures and symbols that represent your main goals.

There are actual computer programs that will send you a message, perhaps popping up on your desktop, which restates your goal.

However you do, you need to be very clear what you main goals are, so you can work on them throughout the day.

Working Within

What does this work consist of?

For one thing, various of ways of focusing internally on what you want. Here are certain ways that people who believe in the importance of framing goals in one's mind and feeling is critical to success:

Saturating Yourself with Positive Media

To move forward as a person does require some kind of intellectual effort. In fact besides that reality that you are what you eat, you also are what you read, what you listen to, and what you watch. To this end, are you reading motivational books, absorbing positive podcasts, studying subjects in your field of interest or in your profession?

The thing about all this discernment about your real desires, setting goals, aligning yourself with Source is that you are trying to correct your thinking.

In the New Testament, the word for repentance is *metanoia*, which comes from the Greek word, *meta*, which means change, and the Greek word for mind, which is *nous* (noia is derived from *nous*). In fact when you are changing your thoughts to conform to Source, you are actually trying to change your thoughts to work with a different part of yourself, which we might call Higher Mind, or what the New Testament calls "spirit," that part of you which is connected to Source or God.

I mentioned books before, the right kind of books, can help connect you to the right way of thinking. And believe me, changing your way of thinking can be a monumental effort, and reading can reinforce and foster that conscious changing of your mind.

But I think in the end, multi-media saturation is best and more fun. In other words, go at changing your thoughts every which way.

• • • • •

What does it mean to "change your mind," or rather change the type of mind you are using (based on being rooted in lower personality in many areas), so that you can align yourself with Source?

• • • • •

Despite the proliferation of all kinds of multi-media, books travel into your mind at whatever pace you set them. They allow you to read and ponder and come back to certain areas if you wish to ponder more.

Start with books, but don't end with multi-media. Keep reading!

• • • • •

What kind of media, in addition to books, do you use to improve your understanding of your product and professional niche, to improve your motivation, to directly improve your salesmanship?

• • • • •

Blogs, often by authors, can reinforce the wisdom in their books. So you can reinforce the lessons you are learning that deal with motivation and directly with upgrading specific your professional skills.

The market rewards patterns of success. There is no secret to success. All the great guys and gals who have succeeded and are succeeding will readily teach it in their books and podcasts.

Learn and do

Learn and do

Learn and do

•   •   •   •   •

Is there a shortage of literature helping you in this direction? How much investigation have you done to find media to help you?

•   •   •   •   •

Many people have chosen these days to spend part of their time in a car listening to audiotapes. This can be a rather important, transformational time.

The amount of material nowadays on YouTube is staggering, pointing to a lot of opportunities to quickly tune into videos that can be a big help in moving you forward.

•   •   •   •   •

> **In what sense has any of this media improved your alignment with your primary goals and mission?**

. . . . .

Visualization

Visualizing the results flowing from main goal should be easy because what you visualize is what you want. So you can imagine receiving the promotion, the diploma, the new job, the community recognition, the new or improved relationship, etc. This experience of receiving this goal should be aligned with the feeling of "rightness" when you first chose it as one of your main goals. Alignment with Source is vital to attain real manifestation.

A tremendous amount of literature nowadays involving visualization emphasizes that you should visualize something as already having happened, as though the goal you are visualizing has in the past, at least in your mind, reached the final state. It's almost as though you are remembering it.

Affirmations

The path to manifestation in any kind of inner path is not totally easy. In my view, affirmation, repeating short phrases over and over, can help perfect your journey.

For instance, if you are not happy with your work, you could say-

I attract a well-paying, exciting job with a great boss and great colleagues, a job that exactly suits my interests and my talents.

Meditation and Prayer

Focusing on Source can be accomplished in many different ways, but meditation and prayer are the traditional ways. It says in the New Testament, "Seek Ye First the Kingdom of God- and its Righteousness and all will be granted to you."

Perhaps reason for the fall, however you take it, symbolically or literally, is that man fell away from our Creator.

I believe you can return by putting it foremost in your thoughts and listen. And by doing this, you bring yourself closer to a point in your life where you can receive actual guidance for your efforts in manifestation.

. . . . .

Do you practice visualization, affirmations, meditation, or prayer? What have been the results of practicing one or more of these options for increasing alignment or clarity of vision?

. . . . .

Execution

Being able to focus or pay attention on whatever you do is a critical skill you are going to reach any particular monetary goal.

Learning is great, and practicing is necessary, but practice alone does not make things perfect. Perfect practice makes perfect approaches. Ask anyone who has learned to fly a plane. The instructor is there to maneuver in safety of flight situations. So it goes that you should look to get adequate ground school under your belt before you fly.

And if you are like my husband, who soloed after five flights with an instructor, then you will be able to ramp up your vocational remuneration much quicker, too.

Some of us are slow starters. I am. So what? Once I get moving on something, I'm like a steamroller. By consciously focusing on the patterns of success for the desired income streams I wish to develop, I can move forward with measured adjustments.

• • • • •

Of course execution based on what you have learned is the whole enchilada. What have you executed so far in regards to conscious selling as outlined in this book, and what changes do you think you will make now you have gotten this far in your reading of White Hat Sales?

• • • • •

Narratives About Money

Yes, I have also heard this:

But, Sandra, I don't care about money. So why should I go to all this trouble?

Really? What is this narrative all about?

You don't have any people on earth who could benefit from the success within you? Any parents? Any children? Or are you saying you really would just like to sleep in and do what ever you want all day? Isn't that just another way of saying you want someone to be responsible for you without hindering your free will?

Money is just a minimum measurement of success.

You will always be setting goals. As you are working towards one set of goals, the universe of possibilities will open farther and wider than you could have imagined.

If you think this doesn't apply to you – look around. Why does your purse get it's own seat?

It's impossible to go to church, the airport, or the mall without a seat being taken up by someone's purse.

I really enjoy fashion. But giving space to an object over the value of human connectedness is taking it a little too far. Is your purse more important than me? In 2020 we gave each other so much space, we found the disfunction and isolation to be harmful mentally. Duh!

Really? We donate thousands of dollars a year to save trees and pets, and you don't care about me? What we all want is to be cared about.

Some would go so far as to say women don't like women. I see it as a selfish pattern of behavior. Perhaps learned in junior high. Fortunately for me, I didn't feel like I fit in well during junior high, and my father showed me skills with sports, animals, and machinery while I developed enough self confidence to make more friends at school.

Team sports for girls growing up does more for women than we really know. It gives us the opportunity to experience organic team work in a dynamic atmosphere. Sound like life? You bet. The common denominator is everyone on earth has faced change. It is how we react and grow that will determine if we excel or fall.

• • • • •

What is your attitude towards making money? Do you think things in this area of concern need to be adjusted?

• • • • •

Paying Attention

Ironically I don't see millennials being so captivated by some of their behavior patterns that will shut them out of top-notch sales. They seem to be the best critics of a status quo that has offered them absolutely no benefit. They have skills, but they would be particularly attracted by the kind of sales that offers residual rewards.

Bravo! Long-term growth and potential means your effort survives your current work.

In sales, if there is no royalty or residual value to your effort, then you are just punching a clock. I believe that's why so many salespeople burn out.

Mindfulness is a great tool because it helps you to pay attention. And paying attention in the sales process has many benefits.

• • • • •

> I have found that the more I pay attention, i.e., be mindful of what I am doing, the more I succeed in my efforts. Have you? And if not, are you willing to try harder by applying the principles and suggestions in this book?

• • • • •

When is all this going, why would you wait for someone to tell you what is going on when you are the one out there toe-to-toe with the consumers? Go for it! With booya! This phrase reminds me what I always believe the steer is thinking when standing in the middle of the field just after climbing the fence surrounding what I previously believed was only freshly mowed field.

Can I run faster to the other side before he charges? Or do I matter less than the fly on his back side being swatted by his tail? He's looking at me in such a way as it could go either way.

I love it. Because if I catch my breath and watch if his head moves, then I have my first indication of my next move. Watch the animal's head. That's where they are going. You can grab a cow or a horse by the nose and turn them away from you. Their head always follows their nose. Their body always follows their head.

That literally could save your life one day, too!

It's like watching the ball and not the player but where the player is moving the ball. Always watch the ball. Player Fake 101 is the best way to maneuver as a youngster. And the negotiation fake is the best move as a real player to see if your counterpart has got the ball.

When I want to know if a buyer is really a buyer, who is really ready to buy right now, I ask them what would they do if we found the right house today. Their answer will help me gauge how to adjust my queue of activity to fit their ability and immediacy. I find out what's in their head by asking the right questions for my industry with conversational ease

And ultimately it matters where my head is.

If I know I help others feel successful by playing a role in this market opportunity, then I believe there is going to be a market reward. So I'm simultaneously I'm maneuvering for information, time, degree of success. It is a continuous calculation, a persistent effort to study the environment in which I am working. Making decisions based on the direction of the head of the bull or the direction where the player is moving the ball. Always looking for the right parameter to pay attention to. Sometimes what very few people know about or will find.

Gearing Up to Win

I can teach a two-year old to catch a ball. I have before. Gifted athletes tend to have gifted children. And they can heave stuff across the room at a very young age. Teach them to catch the ball. In the time that it takes to develop this hand-eye coordination in youngsters, you can take the time to develop your own mouth-ear-eye coordination and keep your head on.

It takes twenty-one days to form a habit. It takes three cycles of twenty-one days to form a pattern in your brain that allows for repeatable thought processes. Are you ready to engage your ears and eyes twice as much as you engage your mouth?

Teachers teach this to their students in school. Under stress these very teachers will demonstrate a lack of ability to contain their words when they are in an unfamiliar environment. So it goes with all of us.

- That way, if you are ready, then you will do.
- You will study.
- You will become better at your craft.
- You will seek the advice of people who are better than you.
- You will surround yourself with people who have patterns of success in your desired field.
- You will dedicate yourself to all options that open the doors to your goals.
- You will take an extra job to pay your bills if your options don't present the remuneration to cover your obligations.

SCREETCH! DID I JUST LOSE YOU?

If you reached for the Cheeto between the couch right now instead of the job postings for night jobs in your area, you might need to read *What Color Is Your Parachute* again. Be in the right sales position that brings you passion. And you can translate that passion to your audience.

Can you do something for a short time, knowing you don't have to do it for the rest of your life? Like one or two extra jobs while you develop the skills, patterns, and performance needed to move up to the next pay level?

Building in a short-term buffer helps keep you from being desperate while you going about your primary pursuit. It also gives you a different exposure to opportunity.

I don't exactly know how it works. But it does. Avenues can open up when you are willing, able, and actually do take on an extra job when you need the money.

Yes, it also means to stop spending. Household finances don't crumble because of cash flow. They crumble because of cash management.

When crisis management and cash management can come together, you can make lemonade out of a very sour financial lemon.

At these moments, you must get focused and be willing to exchange your hard-earned currency for needed items. No more opera tickets or sports skiing in the Alps. Believe me, when you are working two to three, you understand the meaning of the phrase HARD-EARNED. With the right goals, it's always worth it. And it won't last forever.

Don't blab to your friends and daytime co-workers. They may be the very ones who become extremely jealous of your new skills. Your new freedom. Your new pay advantage.

• • • • •

> **What are you willing to do to make yourself a winner? Are you ready to make the steps to catch up on your bills, make more of an effort to study your profession, acquire better counselors, work harder in order to achieve the goals that your own true nature longs for?**

• • • • •

Examine Your Potential

What is your true market value? Research what the current exchange of value is for what you are offering. Each threshold has to do with supply, demand, skill, and timing.

Growing up there was a big demand for newspaper carriers who could skillfully launch a paper from our bag to your front porch. When the snow came in Iowa, the previously able carriers were absorbed by their couch, and the rest of us earned enough money to pay for college in six years.

The snow represented an awesome chance to shovel snow. Good timing here meant getting up in the morning and knocking on doors of my known sphere of opportunity. If I slept in or went sledding, someone else got the job. Maybe even for the rest of the winter. Usually I did all three. Shovel sidewalks. Deliver the paper, then go sledding.

Now that I live in Florida, I see a tremendous opportunity for youngster to mow lawns. I did every summer in Iowa.

Every new capable service team who comes into the market is quickly absorbed. They buy new trucks, boats, houses, horsed, planes, hangers, tugs, and toys because of it. The streets are paved with gold in America. But for some who are so used to walking on them, they don't see the brilliance of opportunity every morning.

At your employment, are you over-worked, under-appreciated? Is that common for this occupation? Or just happening to you because this just isn't the right place for you to work. The unexamined life is not worth living, and the unexamined job is not worth having.

Look at what your doing. Probe. Look at the rewards and weigh them against other possibilities. Stare up at the sky and reach for it as high as you can.

• • • • •

> Are you willing to take advantage of the still rich opportunities American culture offers? Are you will to evolve a strategy that can cope with various possibilities for economic, climatic, military, and other types of social and political changes in your world? No matter what the challenge is, we believe that the solutions lie within ourselves.

• • • • •

END NOTES

1. Mark S. Granovetter, "Getting a Job," (Chicago: University of Chicago Press, 1974, 1995)

2. Gregg Braden, *The Spontaneous Healing of Belief: Shattering the Paradigm of False Limits*, (Carlsbad, California: Hay House, 2008),

3. Ibid, iii

Chapter 10

CREATING A FOLLOWING

A following is a group of people, sometimes identified as "fans," a "following," a "tribe," or "connections" who relate directly to your business and personal activities through various means, like speaking engagements, blogs, social media, in forums and discussion groups, in podcasts, and radio, television, etc. Sometimes this is through a subscription as on the YouTube channel or to a newsletter or through becoming a friend or member in various social media channels. There are numerous ways to do this, and as I write, new ways to connect with technology are being created as old ways are evolving.

Where Do You Put All Those Connections?

Recently I attended an online Writer's Workshop in Hay House, one of the most successful publishers of motivational books, which was founded by one of my author heroines, who I have mentioned before, Louise Hay.

In this workshop, the various contributing authors and representatives of Hay House like Reid Tracy, its CEO, emphasize the importance of what is now called the Author's Platform, the basic foundation of an outreach to a tribe or following. And one of the books they actually give to every attendee at their live workshops is called *Platform: Get Noticed in a Noisy World* by Michael Hyatt.[1] It is published by Thomas Nelson, purportedly the largest Christian publisher in the world, which Michael served as CEO and now Chairman. Most critical for his credentials to write this book is that his leadership blog, as he reports in the introduction, has more than 400,000 monthly visitors and he has more than 50,000 followers subscribing to his daily post. Adding to this, he has more than 100,000 Twitter and 15,000 Facebook followers. In other words, his following is something like a small city.[2]

So when Michael writes about creating a platform, he is not exactly a novice. When he says platform, however, he is not just talking about a platform for authors, but for anyone who has something to say or anyone has a product (or service) to sell. Like the Hay House authors warning Workshop attendees about the necessity for an author's platform, Michael warns salespersons, artists, public speakers, politicians, anyone who is promoting themselves or their product that nothing will work without a platform.

> A good product does not stand on its own anymore. It is foundational, but it is not enough. The answer to the second question is yes. You will need to be proactive about creating the "who" part of the equation. In order for you to be successful in today's business environment, you need two things: a compelling product and a significant platform.[3]

• • • • •

There are many choices for a salesperson, depending on who you are and what you sell. You will have to construct your own platform just like you will have to design, assist, or present your own sales pitch and presentations. We can counsel you on some rules and directions, but even when we begin our workshops or webinars to do that, we will be mainly interested in teaching you the basic protocols.

And you may not be able to do one alone. It can require contact with speaking bureaus, web designers, videographers, freelance writers, graphic designers, etc.

· · · · ·

> What has changed in our economy, the economy itself, technology, communication protocols that demands that a good product no longer can be successfully promoted with conventional media and PR? Why are we compelled to develop a large and sturdy media platform?

· · · · ·

Hopefully before reading on, you have formulated an answer to the above question. If not, before you read on, I suggest you do think about it and possibly scribble down your answer. Why? Because you are talking about a phenomenon, an Internet-based platform which is an entirely new technology of communication and of sales. And you should think about it.

If You Tried to Formulate an Answer, Read On
Here's My Answer

The Internet is the fastest way to promote a product. After all social networks are free. But the reality is that with so many businesses and their representatives entering into the fray, soon social media advertising, for many, became a vital part of the process and the cost of its creation, which now often demanded sophisticated graphics, animation, video, etc. placed another burden on those wishing to promote products. Further, of course after a bit of time, major businesses entered into that domain as well. Look how the Internet has pushed away the dominance of so many brick and mortar businesses, hard copy newspapers and bookstores. And look at the obsession, and sometimes necessary obsession, for people to utilize social media and the Internet. Traditional media is still powerful though but is dominated by major companies. So technology, the economy, dominated by a relatively small number of major players and communication protocols, all play a role.

On the other hand, the Platform is an opportunity for immense creativity and self-expression, a chance to personalize your business and the space to say whatever you want in a relatively unrestricted way.

Your platform will ultimately develop by you for the purpose of conducting White Hat Sales, but it will need to be exquisitely customized to your own personality, product, or service. It also involves a continually emerging technology of which, for the moment, social media is probably the most conspicuous, but webinars and other opportunities for webcasting programs, both served by Google Hangouts, Go to Meeting, and other such programs, become increasingly critical.

Of course as a White Hatter, you will probably want to promote your affiliation with the ideals and purposes of these blogs. Ultimately when we develop our workshops and training programs, we will probably offer some kind of certification and a pledge to do good things with your sales talents and the fine products you represent.

• • • • •

What kind of a platform for sharing your product or service do you have? Is it good enough? If you have one, what could you do to enhance it? If you don't, how would you like it designed?

• • • • •

The Internet: Different Choices for Different Voices

No matter what you do in business these days, you generally have to be positioned on the Internet, hopefully with an audience that really wants to hear what you say. Of course if you work for a large retail store selling say cosmetics, your involvement in the Internet may be quite marginal. Your audience finds you because of the prestige of the source and the tremendous power of its massive advertising and promotion.

Then again if you are some type of commissioned salesperson or member of a cosmetically oriented multi-level company who regularly does makeovers as part of her job in selling cosmetics, you may definitely want to have an Internet presence. You may need to draw people towards you, perhaps by online advertising and social media.

Just to carry the point a bit further, an upscale hair stylist or massage therapist who works for a large company may be more or less dependent on company advertising to bring her business, but if she's independent and pays for her own booth in a salon or, in the case of the masseuse, a room in a chiropractic facility or health spa, the website and other Internet-based components may be vital to her success.

Though relatively simple retail sales jobs in a well-advertised and trafficked physical area may not need a following to support their sales, many of the principles of White Hat Sales may still apply. And if the retail worker does a good job, she will get referrals from satisfied clients and that will help her relationship to her employer. This also is a following.

• • • • •

> In what way should you be using the Internet as a sales practitioner, keeping in mind the type of sales platform may differ widely depending on what you actually sell?

· · · · ·

> What kind of sales practitioner needs to have a very heavy, complex platform, and what kind of practitioner can have a somewhat or very much simpler platform? How does what you sell and who you are help define the nature of your platform?

· · · · ·

The Primacy of Referrals

Perhaps one of the most important things to do, if you are successful with a client, is to ask for referrals. I do this during the Escrow stage of my work. As things approach a happy ending, this is the time to build your business on the foundations you have created.

· · · · ·

> At this present moment, how important have referrals been in building your business? How can you incorporate an enhanced search for referrals in your live contacts and online?

• • • • •

In social media, referrals can be developed in many ways. One of the strongest is called "sharing."

This is the opposite of scarcity mentality. This is a sharing which helps all of us mentally. The more deposits I make with relevant content, the more you benefit. Do so when you engage in social media is important, too. The more your social network benefits, the greater the opportunity you will have in becoming engaged in a transaction with me and my product or service.

• • • • •

In terms of networking, prior to reading the foregoing, did you look at people in similar fields as competitors or as potential allies?

• • • • •

"Sharing" means re-tweeting or reposting social media messages in a variety of venues. My main emphasis here is on LinkedIn, Facebook, Twitter, and YouTube. This means that when you receive a worthwhile message from someone you want as an ally, you may first join them as a member or a follower in a specific social media (or several) and then later share their messages with others in your specific network.

Deposit. Deposit. Deposit. If your deposits are fodder, inferior, and readily available, then the laws of reciprocity will demonstrate themselves. You'll have nothing of value to show for your time.

• • • • •

Sandra E. LaFlamme

> For instance, when you make a sale, when is the best time to ask for a referral? Also, when you post or tweet something online, do you ask for it to be shared? Furthermore how much sharing do you actually offer in your networks and with your clients, who might also need referrals for their business?

• • • • •

Social Media Is Great But–
Not All Followers are Influencers

For anyone who has a large network like I do, you know how impossible it is to deal with everyone. From a personal perspective, of course deal with anyone you really want to know, make friends and worthwhile associates, and take advantage of the personal or social side of a social network. Whatever number that is, if you sincerely want to communicate with people effectively, those close ties will probably nowhere near the number of people you need in your network.

• • • • •

> Do you already especially target influencers in your networks; i.e., people with large networks that can help you sell your product or service? If so, how do you do this? What can you do to attract more influencers?

• • • • •

Social Networks- The White Hat Way

What would be the White Hat way to master LinkedIn, Facebook, Twitter, YouTube, and some of the others? I believe the first criteria is your choice of a product that works, you believe in, and whose price can be easily understood, that reflects the integrity of a true sales practitioner. The second criteria is authenticity, a quality we have covered previously in regards to personal sales.

Authenticity is important to all sales but much more difficult to project in websites, social media, bulk email, radio, TV, and other forms of advertising. The way you write, the way you speak, the way you look to an unknown, outside audience should ring of, shall we say, "truth in advertising," not just intellectual truth but emotional truth, integrity.

But in all of the so-called social networks I have mentioned, there is also distinctly a business side. That business side demands looking carefully for the people who will assist you in selling their product. And those are people who generally have thousands of followers and who are willing to share with you.

In most high-ticket sales, for instance, it would require a way to identify real prospective buyers and gradually convert them from distant to medium to close ties where they might really approachable for a sale. As one example, the subtle use of discussion groups using the guideline of preserving authenticity of purpose is a way to begin that type of connection.

These people often built their following by sharing with other people. But probably not everyone. Rather with people who had large networks and who fit into their framework of appropriate contacts.

To find influencers beyond those you already know, you need to search for them and follow them. After following them, you can reach out to them, often by offering them something more than reposting, maybe a show in your podcast or an article in your newsletter. Or maybe if the situation is right, a heart-to-heart talk about a subject of mutual concern in Skype or a discussion of some topic on the phone. Or even an outright solicitation of their help and an offer for some kind reciprocal but completely customized help.

For instance if you are a speaker with wide contacts in various speaking bureaus, you could give them some vital contacts, or if you are an author, you could ask them to write an introduction to your book. Even if you are an emerging mass networker, you may find something that is meaningful for them.

· · · · ·

> **How do you convert or plan on connecting medium or low ties on social networks (where people respectively some- what or hardly know you) to close ties (where you are ac- tively engaging with them)?**

· · · · ·

And speaking of meaningful, as someone who practices networking daily, *meaningful*, both live (with actually flesh-and-blood Clients) and online in a variety of networks, I don't do "trite," "babble," or simple self-serving obsessional outreaches. In the past, I have created writing products that actually help people, particularly realtors, and I do the same in my speaking engagements. I started because I wanted to help people, and like other business people when it comes to the career side of my life, people who I can help, often realtors like myself, increase their sales and profitability.

But now my goals have expanded from helping realtors, to helping sales people in general, as my experience is broader than just luxury homes sales and I think I can be of value for sales people in general. You can truthfully say that this book, *White Hat Sales*, is doing just that and writing books and creating certain types of workshops and programs is part of my forthcoming platform.

· · · · ·

> **Why is it really important to communicate meaningfully with people, both personally, in limited, or mass media?**

· · · · ·

Websites – A Basic Component of Your Platform

For most people, a following means building a powerful presence on the Internet. In most cases, if you sell a product(s) (or service), you will need a a Facebook page or business website devoted to that product or product line. For people like myself (I work for a broker as a realtor), the company provides me and other employees like myself with a profile in their large and well-promulgated website.

If you are working for a multi-level company or as an affiliate of a company, you may likely have a clone of the company website with certain embedded codes, so that when a product is purchased, your commission is recorded or even disbursed.

A business website of a company will often have to be search-engine optimized, so that you can benefit from search engine results. Often companies will invest in ad words or pay-by-click advertising, which will pull up ads related to search engine inquiries at the top of the first page or adjacently on the side of the page. No doubt this kind of advertising is very complex, involving the selection of keywords that are balanced against competitors for popularity, which influences cost, and the effectiveness of the ad itself. Another aspect of websites and other forms of Internet marketing is Search Engine Optimization or SEO. This is an attempt to register higher on Google (and other browsers perhaps) when certain strategically chosen keywords are punched in. SEO can be used for blogs, press releases, articles, and other components of Internet promotion.

Both SEO and ad words advertising can be expensive and tricky. Simply purchasing these services can be valuable or a complete waste of time, mainly because it is a very technical and artful kind of advertising and mechanical, non-intuitive expertise does not work very well in this kind of promotion. Fortunes are made in advertising because of intuitive, creative outreaches to the public that does not necessarily fit into any kind of standardized playbook.

· · · · ·

> What kind of shape are your websites? Are your websites being visited? In addition to a business site, do you have a personal branding website? In your case, in addition to your business efforts, should your personality or reputation be given special attention in your promotions?

· · · · ·

I bring this up because many of my readers are small business people whose success depends on their sales, and sometimes in very small companies, this means the sales efforts of their owners.

Sometimes the sales or leads for sales from the company website will be doled out to its sales agents, so even though you might not have much input or even the slightest profile in the website, it is serving you for sales.

You Probably Need A Platform

It is quite true that there are some people whose company really does almost all the work they need on their major platform. These people just have to plug in some information and a picture or two into a company website.

But even if you have a company website doesn't mean you can't go farther to social profiles, to a personal branding site, to your own podcasting program, to your own out reach to appropriate organizations, networking clubs, or online forums or discussion group to further extend your platform.

It might be worth it to make the extra effort.

END NOTES

1. Michael Hyatt Platform: Get Noticed in a Noisy World. (Nashville, Tennesee: Thomas Nelson, 2012). Kindle Edition.

2. Ibid.

3. Ibid., Location 331

Appendix

WHITE HAT SALES PROTOCOLS
The Keys to Accelerating Sales Success

PROTOCOL #1
AUTHENTICITY

Our first and absolute protocol is authenticity.

Every human being on Earth is different. We are like snowflakes, widely different in our designs but all floating towards our destination on the Earth together but in a slightly different location from each other.

White Hat Sales is not a cookie cutter factory for making sales practitioners. Sales practitioners have a dedicated role, to present and sell products and/or services. This means they are enmeshed in and responsible for a great deal of data about what they are selling, regardless of their personalities and their intentions. This means that they have to convey that data to the customers, we hope in a highly customized way and in a way that complements their own individuality.

In fact, as we have pointed out, we want you to be authentic in every detail of your job. As an example, certainly specific aspects of a presentation might have to be memorized or at least remembered, but even this type of material should be so well-assimilated, understood, and believed in as the truth that it comes off as the authentic person you really are. You should believe in what you present because it is true and beneficial to your client. Period.

Have you ever heard a customer service person at a bank or a sales person on the phone pretend they are delivering some kind of flowery, well-articulated speech about how glad they were to be of service to you and how excited they are to present a cavalcade of benefits for you out of this amazing product or service they are about to present to you? Have you, while hearing them, suppressed an urge to either laugh or maybe throw up because it was so blatantly obvious that they were the poorly supervised representative of a scriptwriter for a company who wanted to manipulate customers by guiding their thoughts, words, and intentions through their well-constructed scripts.

Since we are the White Hat Sales non-robotic salesperson Division of the LaFlamme Advanced Communication Training program, we advocate scripted sales to cover important questions of technical precision, conformity to legal necessities, or for the clarity of financial terms and conditions. Without contextual understanding of clients's goals and needs the script will fail. Therefore, as mentioned previously, we always want our salespeople to be themselves, and this means speaking in their own voice, as much as possible.

But, yes, if you write and customize a script and can deliver it with a feeling that corresponds to the way you felt when you created it, it is for some, quite necessary.

Always, communication means making accommodations to the client, vendor, or manager. This can mean assuming a somewhat different personae and is allowable, if you have to be extra sweet to an older man or woman, if you have to gruff or even appearing threatening to someone trying to pull the wool over your eyes as in an attempt in outright deception or fraud, if you have to be overly-courteous to a client who is absolutely in the wrong but would never admit it. In these circumstances, you may in fact be acting a part, but it can be an act of authenticity because your "act" is required because of legitimate self-defense, compassion, or to be able to communicate at all.

As Polonious says to his son Laertes in Shakespeare's *Hamlet*:

This above all: to thine own self be true,
And it must follow, as the night the day,
Thou canst not then be false to any man.

This very much could be the slogan of the White Hat Sales training program.

Be true to thyself. You will sleep better at night.

PROTOCOL #2
KNOWING THE PRODUCT

It would seem a truism that a salesperson should know their product. But the reality is- many don't, at least not efficiently enough to maximize their potential. For many if there is a product line with multiple components, they only know some of their products. Sometimes they miss knowing about the very products in their line that the client might need. You can say good-bye for sales that miss products that exist in the line but are never identified by salespeople who stress the minimal in the examination of their own inventory.

As we have pointed out, drawing from the Challenger model we have discussed previously, sometimes it is best that a sales practitioner knows the product so well that they can produce innovative customized solutions for the client that is not present in generalized sales presentation or advertising and that the client would never have thought of on their own. This can produce the development of a unique and coveted relationship between the sales representative and the purchasing company, which means recurring sales and prestige for the company selling the product.

PROTOCOL #2A
KNOWING THE PRODUCT PLACEMENT

Knowing the business of your product sales component is the professional approach to profitability. What is the profit margin and profit percentage of your product? What are your volume bonus breakpoints? What is its shelf life? What is the absorption rate of the current inventory – establishing net present value? What place to you occupy in the marketplace?

If you are the selling agent for the only hut on the island and there are four families looking for a place to live, then you have a captive audience that will present themselves in the order in which they self determine their needs and their means.

Acknowledging the opportunity for back orders, competition for those orders gives you insight into current value and future value of your inventory. And future opportunity.

PROTOCOL #3
FULL DISCLOSURE ABOUT PRODUCT

Ever buy a car, perhaps from a private party, and find that despite the assurances and engaging rapport with the seller, the engine began to overheat on a regular basis? Well, you bought the car, signed some kind of a non-return agreement, and you now have repairs ahead that equal or surpass that of the car's price.

It would be a horrendous job to try and document, even with one line per situation, the number of problems that occur to consumers with regards to non-disclosure on a daily basis throughout this country. Probably in the millions.

Recently a friend was looking for some OCR software to optically scan some documents. He found one that had literally mouth-watering claims, which might have quashed the doubts of almost anyone who was really suspicious of claims about this kind of software, having been grievously disappointed before.

Still at first all looked well. The software promised to do any kind of typical scan, including pre-scanned pdfs and there were multiple positive in-house statements about the software.

Then he looked at the terms, a portion of a sales website he often ignored and found that the fabulous refund policy demanded that you had read the product description carefully in advance. Also, you had to somehow prove to the company you had a firm grasp of the technical challenges involved in OCR software. Indeed if you did not understand what you read, according to the company, there would be no refund. If you made a mistake purchasing a wrong product and then purchased a right product, there would be no refund. Whoa!

Now, in this case, there was a rather complete disclosure of these and other terms of the refund- but who generally reads this? Many companies have rather unconditional terms for refunding software purchases.

After seeing these terms, my friend looked at outside reviews and found multiple and sometimes angry statements about this software. The company follow-up on complaints, in some cases, was claimed to be non-existent.

Sometimes non-disclosure can occur with large print as it does so often in small print. A lot of this has to do with a company understanding consumers' expectations. If they believe that they can disclose a problem without the consumer statistically likely to notice, then this is a Gray Hat method of non-disclosure. They disclosed, knowing fully that only a few consumers would realize what they had said. Legally compliant, ethically a disgrace.

We fully disclose in White Hat Sales, even though as with any type of product or service, this can be awkward. Yes, we could lose the sale or have to return the money.

PROTOCOL #4
LOCATING THE PRODUCT

If someone wants to buy an ancient California bungalow or locate a specific type Formica kitchen counter or find a Firmstrong beachbike for a little girl in a huge bicycle warehouse, a salesperson may have to help. Helping identify a needed or desired item may be the first way you relate to a customer, and it is critical.

Let me give you a really simplistic example.

If you go into some large grocery stores, the ones with inadequate signage, and you ask to find something, you may be forced to seek out some kind of help to find the product. I said this was simplistic, one of the first things about a product that makes it useful, is that you can find it, especially in a grocery store when you are in a hurry.

And most people, after a few minutes of looking, will abandon their search instead of creating a hunter/gatherer mentality and spending the next three hours looking for specific laundry cleaner or a gourmet frozen breaded Italian meatball dish.

But when you ask where the product is in a large grocery store, there are a number of options. One they will say they don't know and vaguely point to a cashier or some other clerk or tell you to go somewhere without specifying the location, except in a general way. Two, they may directly tell you, "It's on aisle three, on the left hand side, almost directly in the middle of the aisle." And then there are some stores where the clerk, the packer, the cashier, anyone who actually works there will stop what they're doing and say, "No problem. Just come with me." They will then walk over to the shelf and maybe even hand you the product.

This is the Ritz Carlton Gold Standards style of service. In their list of ten service values, #3 states clearly, "I am always responsive the expressed and unexpressed wishes and needs of our guests."

This protocol is all about responsiveness to the expressed "wishes and needs" of one's customers. If they ask, you try and deliver if it is humanly possible. Yes, there is some leeway here, but the major goal on their employees is to "go the distance."

Now apply this to every element of the sales and you have something really going for you.

PROTOCOL #5
KNOW YOUR PRICE STRUCTURE INTIMATELY

It would be nice if all price structure were truly one-price-for-all. Then you could go to car lot, and no matter what cars were there, there would be a standard price. Of course that will never happen. If so you would miss the hours of futile negotiations on sales lots, often leaving after the final price is reached with the realization that somehow you have lost a lot of pieces off your shirt and most likely the whole thing. Much of this usually takes place at the end of the sale when you talk to the financial officer who reveals certain aspects of the sale that were never mentioned before.

The fact is many clients are price-obsessed at the very beginning of the sale. They want to get over this naughty price business as soon as possible and they need that reassurance to function properly.

The problem with certain pricing structures is that they can be amazingly complex, and if there are a lot of products or services with choices as to the preferred one, there can be difficulties in really learning all this and being ready to spout it out on a moment's call. Nonetheless it is my opinion that this structure needs to be known, probably memorized with the varying choices per product intact in your consciousness.

I call taking care of price considerations that come up spontaneously and prematurely by the client *price therapy*. This is not to be confused with continual, random closing techniques. The point here is not to use this pricing information as a club but as a form of assurance to the client.

Price therapy means to reveal as much as you can to the client whenever he asks and explain carefully what you cannot reveal, principally because all the elements of the product or service have not been decided on, or since payment may involve terms, this may have to be calculated later or even by another person. Kindness and a willingness not to be pushy are requirements for price therapy to work. Also, you must be willing to accept that the client may find the product or service truly unaffordable, and you must be ready to let him walk away. Still if the customer doesn't "get" the facts you are presenting and is making decisions unreasonably, you may have to persevere. It is your job to inform completely and help him make a rational decision, if you can. Helping them have closure is closing each step of the way toward the transaction.

PROTOCOL #6
HANDLING OBJECTIONS THE WHITE HAT WAY

Speaking of the last example, it may well be, as I have indicated, that the only closing will be the client getting up to leave when he hears the price, thus short circuiting the sales presentation.

My answer to the concerned practitioner who experiences this "closure" is the same advice old school salesmen might say to the novice sales guy. "Remember what the bank teller says when the customer is finished his banking experience at the teller window, NEXT!"

The serious practitioner will be delighted not to waste his time, assuming the customer is leaving because the price of the sale is truly beyond his means. Now he has the time to deal with another prospect, repeat customer, or prospecting/promotional activities to bring the next person to the table. NEXT is good! (Sometimes)

PROTOCOL #7
LEGALITIES

In certain types of sales, the legalities mean almost nothing. A retail sales clerk in a clothing store may never have to deal with any official legalities, only the protocols and policies of his company. In other types of sales, like mine, real estate, there are many laws to contend with, safety, contractual, zoning, taxation, fraud, fiduciary responsibilities, anti-trust laws, misleading advertising, fair housing regulations, legal criteria for settlements, limitations on anything resembling legal advice that could represent unauthorized practice of law, disability laws, etc.

Some salespeople, once they are aware of the legalities involved in their business, feel they could literally drown in their company's sea of rules and regulations, so their response is to avoid drowning and ignore doing their job of knowing where vendor and consumer rights and responsibilities are.

This is a big mistake. Not only does a White Hat practitioner need to know about their product, but they also need to know about the laws that govern their particular form of transactions.

PROTOCOL #8
SELL EMPATHICALLY

Always try and "tune in" to your customers. This may require you by-passing your own needs to influence their behavior and putting your attention by stepping into their shoes and finding out what they want, what they need, and the exact nature of their reflective and reflexive thinking in the context of the sales, as best you can interpret it.

If you are not naturally empathic prior to reading this book, then I will ask you to prepare every major presentation by, in part, reminding yourself to be empathic.

Remember the Ritz Carlton pledge we just discussed:

I am always responsive to the expressed and unexpressed wishes and needs of our guests. This protocol allows you to focus on the "unexpressed wishes and needs" of the customer.

How can something unexpressed be identified? Let me tell you, it takes concentration. Sometimes it is through body knowledge, seeing that someone is feeling uncomfortable, perhaps fidgeting because what is being said, say the price of the product again is making them uncomfortable or something as simple as shivering because the air conditioner in the room you are selling in is way too high. Many times it is through their tone of voice at times as they try to mask their dissatisfaction and sometimes when it is clear as a bell. Sometimes, however, it is the unarticulated admiration in their voice after they have seen the house, gone on the tour, spent some time alone in the showroom, etc. Being responsive to this unspoken clue could result in a mammoth sale.

PROTOCOL #9
BUILD RELATIONSHIPS

We agree with the Challenger Sale clarification of the importance of innovative product knowledge and an almost intuitive sense of what your company or product/service inventory might have that the client doesn't know about, particularly in big corporate sales. In fact in any kind of sales, product knowledge and contextual thinking is always important.

But still regardless of what priorities you might put on your sales activities, we regard all our protocols as being of prime importance if applicable or possible in a sales situation.

In certain cases, as mentioned, when pitching something to a closed room with largely unknown suits, perhaps well-dressed venture capitalists with strange, shark-like behavior, you may not know them and never have the opportunity of personal involvement with them and have seventeen and a half minutes to talk to them anyway, then this is the time to speak authoritatively quick and avoid relationship building with much small talk...and have a stone cold knowledge that your appearance is relatable.

But in most cases, relationship building should begin at the beginning when you are first introduced to a person. This needn't be too long, and it should be yourself talking, not a robotic, always closing, always pitching professional whose eye is always on the client's pocketbook.

If you are going to engage in empathic sales, you really have to know the person and not just rely on body knowledge or tone of voice to give you a clue as to the client's intention. Clients who are comfortable with you and recognize a desire to truly know them will certainly be more inclined, even casual interchanges, to do business with you. So questions are important to sound conversation all they need to be specifically survey oriented to gain understanding and to drive the fact finding so you exemplify expertise with repoire.

PROTOCOL #10 THE GOAL:
A SALE SUPPORTED BY RATIONAL COMPLIANCE

As I have indicated, we are actually trying to sell something, and there certainly will be a natural enthusiasm and interest in what we are doing, mainly because we believe in it but also of course because more sales is better than less sales. I subscribe to the Biblical injunction, "Love Thy neighbor as Thyself." If this is true, then interactions should be me-win/you-win scenarios. If there is a place for love of others in the universe, there is also room for love of oneself, and perhaps in a way, that is primary because while other relationships may be transient, if one is alive, one is always with oneself.

This protocol somewhat sets us apart from many sales programs that are somewhat based on neuro-science because the intention is good, and to some, may seem self-sacrificing. Yes, in White Hat Sales, we are willing to lose some sales owing to what we have established is based on the best interest of the client. We do not feel that this compromises our long-range possibilities of highly successful sales. This belief is based on the assumption striving for integrity and caution with the client's objectives will conform to a portion of the universal law, which governs the attainment of personal goals.

If the Source of all things is genuine goodness, then mirroring that goodness in our personal behavior will attract the kind of good that we ultimately need to see. In this manner, White Hat Sales draws upon a proven, though not readily popularized, view of the power of alignment with the Source that energizes and draws to us what we need to be successful in our goals.

We are looking for a rational and enlightened consent to purchase.

PROTOCOL #11
THE JUDICIOUS USE OF QUESTIONS

Perhaps the key way to learn about your client is to ask questions and then to follow-up with more questions and relevant conversation about the answers.

Questions can be used in a manipulative way, like, "Can you imagine, with all the problems this country is having with health care that anyone hearing that they had found the perfect way to solve their health concerns for themselves and their family in a perfectly affordable way would ignore that opportunity, particularly if there was a government-designated deadline for enrolling?" A nice long question designed to facilitate the sale and shame the customer if he does not buy.

Whether one likes the involvement in government in healthcare or not, even the specific form of involvement, shaming a client into buying something for you to make a profit is generally a rather Black Hat low blow.

PROTOCOL #12
IDENTIFYING THE CLIENT'S NARRATIVE

The way we do this is by trying to construct the framing the client is doing in regards to the prospect of purchasing the object of our selling. Is the client absorbing correctly the information he is being given, or is he reacting favorably or unfavorably to an element in our presentation he has misunderstood? Perhaps the couple has misunderstood the price or the terms of payment; perhaps he has misheard when the house was first constructed or the degree of versatility of the food processor she is considering to buy. Perhaps he is reacting emotionally because he thinks a product is dangerous because he is confusing an ingredient with another chemical compound.

Sometimes nothing is clear until we ask questions based on the tone of voice and demeanor of who we are helping.

PROTOCOL #13 DISCERNING HIDDEN
NARRATIVES WHEN HANDLING OBJECTIONS

Sometimes the client is framing an objection obliquely that doesn't make sense, like the mobile home isn't big enough when it clearly is, or that the rug samples he is seeing have designs, which are too busy for his décor. The sensitive sales practitioner may sense that the hidden narrative is that the client simply can't afford the trailer home or rugs styles he is seeing. If the practitioner senses this, he can possibly help the client to reframe his narrative simply by showing him more affordable samples, like a different trailer or different rug samples without necessarily even questioning the affordability of the object in question.

PROTOCOL #14
REFRAMING THE CLIENT'S NARRATIVE

This is, perhaps, the most subtle and important way we use neuro-science in the White Hat Sales process.

If a client is reactive, or in our opinion, is jumping towards and away from the sale too quickly, using reflexive instead of rational thinking, we want to help put the client back on track.

If someone were just in love with stonework on the façade of a house and the house was very over-priced, as a White Hat practitioner, and there were other houses being considered in a neighborhood critical to the client's interest, I would have to try to temper the client's enthusiasm for the house's appearance with the price of the house that could bind the client to his mortgage for thirty or more years, despite the fact that if I were into manipulative sales, this would be the closing moment.

Yes, as in other types of sales, we do try and build a case for our product, but we do this by creating a foundation of real "yeses" based on the client's true needs, desires, and capabilities.

If a client loves the appearance of the house and it is clouding out the reality of the sale, it is our job to reframe the client's desire for a house with the totality of all the components that would function for a rational decision, for instance the neighborhood, as mentioned in a previous example, the need for repairs, safety factors involved in the current condition and materials used in the house, the history of the house, its future demands on capital for client-based desired for expansion or changes in the house (like adding a room or a patio), the down payment, and other terms of the contract and all the other factors he or she needs to know.

PROTOCOL #15
DO NOT USE COGNITIVE PERSUASION, NEURO-LINGUISTIC PROGRAMMING OR OUTRIGHT DECEPTION TO CREATE SALES

As we have discussed, cognitive persuasion is providing a consumer-winning narrative to the consumer that emphasizes the kind of rosy picture that the human mind, in a non-reflective state, gravitates to.

Car and timeshare sales are the kind of sales that generally benefit from the "closed door effect."

The "closed door effect" refers to an exchange where the parties involved are not open to outside feedback and are, in effect, isolated in their discussion with no real permissible ability to leave. Often this restraint is based on time or etiquette considerations.

The closed-door effect can be created by a sales agent by stressing the extreme demand on the product and that making a quick decision is necessary. In a car transaction, there is often an internal pressure within the consumer's mind to get the deal over with and get the car and go home so the consumer, already weary by the long sales presentation and perhaps wandering all over the lot.

A major manipulation "trick" is to create a sense of demand for the product when there is none in reality to speed up the closing of the sale.

An NLP trick is to use a soft, soothing, conversational tone to actually induce a trance state in the consumer and thereby making him more amenable to a reflexive sales opportunity. We would rather "wake up" a licent and make him think than lull into a light, hypnotic trance.

PROTOCOL #16
CREATING A FOLLOWING

There are a number of ways to achieve a following. Let's talk about three Internet methods: social media, blogs, and email autoresponder recipients. Although to do it the right way can be a bit pricey, in certain cases there is a very small cost. In business these methods are basically used to capture and retain followers, but they are not the only way to recruit them, and hopefully they are more than just cold, hard solicitations but interesting, informative, and carefully targeted to the interests of the recipients. Networking groups, press releases, articles, backlinks in other websites, reciprocal links (where you share links with other websites), speaking engagements, books, webinars, and special Internet promotions, podcasting, webcasting, and various forms of television and radio appearances are ways to create the kind of following that will add to your subscription base, which is the more measurable part of a following.

PROTOCOL #17
GETTING A WEBSITE

Everybody in business needs a Facebook page YouTube or website. If you are in business of a certain kind, you may use your own website, or if not, you may piggyback on your employer's business website. Facebook is where community is formed. YouTube has the highest commercial intent through Google. Your website is for transaction details. For many of us, it is important to have our own personal branding site in our own name, (johnsmith.com). This way if people look us up, they can see a site which shows professional and personal content about our family, friends, hobbies, education with a lot of photos and personal history, a tad more than an "About" page on a website. A glimpse into our soul as far as the Internet can provide. Everything is more personal than ever. So develop your brand that provides transparency, shows enthusiasm while guarding your privacy.

PROTOCOL #18
SOCIAL NETWORKS- REALITY AND ILLUSION

The Internet has spawned social media, which has become a daily obsession for private use, and in many cases, a prerequisite for sales and marketing. Like other developments during the evolution of the Internet, it offers a great deal of promise to many and a perfect realization for relatively few. It can easily create a rather transparent illusion of close ties where none exists, except in being a member of a giant chain of friends or associates relatively unknown contacts. Although with many products and services, a large field of contacts might be recommended, for many the trick is to identify a group with which one can really do business.

PROTOCOL #19
GROW YOUR BUSINESS WITH REFERRALS

As I have pointed out, real business growth related to sales is usually generated by referrals. Grow your business. Memorize and imprint in your brain this perennial truth about the universe, "It Never Hurts to Ask" (Don't forget the capital letters when you write it on your refrigerator and a few of your walls). Social media can create referral with the appropriate use of automation. Automation stemming from your authentic voices gives clients a way to find you, as a White Hatter, quicker and saves them from the opposite experience.

PROTOCOL #20
JOIN LIVE NETWORKING CLUBS, FRATERNAL ORGANIZATIONS, ONLINE DISCUSSION GROUPS AND FORUMS

The world of sales revolves around connections. Let your connections share their connections. Make your connections in any way that seems pleasant and natural but don't fail to make them. Sometimes the best way is to meet and discuss important things with people and put your sales hat on the table. Let people know you and approach them inwardly for other than self-serving interests. So play golf, bowl, visit charity auctions or sporting events, take courses in school, meet and mix with people for personal and educational reasons, and let friendships and then business possibly grow out of that.

PROTOCOL #21
GET ALL THE REST YOU NEED

Everything in life, whether professionally or personally related, can be overdone. If you are going to succeed in White Hat Sales, you need to be prepared to stay on top of your game. Getting enough rest is part of being ready every day to meet the challenges and opportunities you will face.

One time when I was with my mom in a nutritionist's office, she answered a nutritional questionnaire that I looked over. In it she clearly stated that she was sleeping well.

I knew this to be wrong. And she was offended when I called her out in front of the nutritionist. Defending her answer, she said, "Well, for four hours I'm sleeping sound. Then I wake up. Then I go back to sleep. And sleep two more hours. Then I go back to sleep if I can."

If you want to truly be ready to take on the world, you need to have a relative benchmarks for sleep, food, and exercises and to clarify what your goals should be for each situation.

PROTOCOL #22
BENEFICIAL NUTRITION

Nutritional deficiencies can cause loss of sleep. Stress. Deficiency in thought. If you have as many aerobic fitness instructors, massage therapist, compounding pharmacist, nutritionist, colon therapist in your phone as you do hair stylist, then this part is not new to you.

PROTOCOL #23
FOCUS ON WHAT YOU REALLY WANT

If you want to see progress in your life, guard your thoughts against negativity and change your negative narratives, which at least in part control those thoughts.

Also, since this is a blessed universe whenever you maintain the proper connection to its Source, remember that what you truly desire is embedded in that connection.

Therefore always pay attention to and visualize your main goals all the while giving enough focus to visualizing the steps along way

Sandra E. LaFlamme

and the need to overcome specific challenges along the way. For me prayer is also a key part of this process, but I am aware that I have choices to make and act on also. Our inner work on co-operating with the manifestation of our real desires is every bit, if not more, important than what we do externally. Love edifies, knowledge only will puff you up.

It is better that we focus meticulously on both, love most importantly.

Author's Biography

SANDRA LAFLAMME

Sandra LaFlamme was meant to write a book like *White Hat Sales* in the same manner she was inspired to create the *LaFlamme Advanced Communication Training*. She is motivated fundamentally by a love of people and a strong belief that American consumers deserve to work with companies and people who create worthwhile goods and services, which are sold to them with passion and integrity.

"In my lifetime, I have always been interested and involved in selling. But looking across the landscape of products and sales practices in this country, I have seen a great deal of deception practiced by companies and their sales representatives. We now know through breakthroughs in neuroscience that something like 95% of what human beings think is unconscious. Whereas this fact is often used in manipulative sales practices, I think an understanding of the way our minds work can bring a revolution in serving people, even more accurately and responsibly. That's why I inaugurated FLAME and wrote White Hat Marketing, integrity, empathy, and science can all aid in creating prosperity for the company and people willing to engage in a truly high-minded sales process."

Prior to her work as a luxury homes realtor for Coldwell Banker in Sarasota, Florida, an occupation deploying so many of her formidable sales skills, she moved towards her current occupation through a myriad of sales-oriented occupations. She has the experience of working in industrial sales for Pittsburgh paints, selling securities and other financial instruments for TransAmerica, integrating sales objectives for her work in computer training for Altos Origin and Gateway Computers, creating and marketing Manna Properties, a land development company which created and sold twenty-five residential properties and helped orchestrate sales as an owner of Spa413, a medical day spa. In so doing, she has seen many facets of the sales process and has been able to continually reflect and refine her own sales techniques.

As Sandra says about her work, "As a real estate expert and a speaker, my outreach is backed by a powerful combination of rich history and global strength. My sales record of satisfied clients has me as one of the Top Ranked Agents on Trulia with an active involvement as a luxury realtor for over twenty years. As I have pushed forward in my own sales career, I have become more and more concerned about the general nature of marketing and sales in my country. Although I am fully satisfied with my own company's integrity, looking out there, I see a great deal of deceptive and shoddy practices in the real estate market, as well as everywhere else. I feel motivated to do something about this. I guess you might say I want to change the way people look at buying and selling in the American marketplace."

Current, Sarasota Association of Realtors®. 2004 Commercial Real Estate Historic Preservation Award, Newport, KY, 2005 Board Member Northern Kentucky Association of Realtors®, 2005 Education Board Member Darlene Bishop Home for Life, Monroe Ohio.2007-08 Foundation Board for Sarasota Optimist, 2001 Coldwell Banker West Shell Cincinnati Area All Star Rookie Real Estate Agent Team, 1990 - 1994 Board Member Lexington Crisis Center. 1991 Saxony Farm / Lexington KY — Polo Team. 1980 AQHA All Around Youth.